Norman Coe

Grammar Spectrum 3

Intermediate
With answers

Oxford University Press

Oxford University Press
Great Clarendon Street, Oxford OX2 6DP

Oxford New York
Athens Auckland Bangkok Bogotá Buenos Aires
Calcutta Cape Town Chennai Dar es Salaam
Delhi Florence Hong Kong Istanbul Karachi
Kuala Lumpur Madrid Melbourne Mexico City
Mumbai Nairobi Paris São Paulo Singapore
Taipei Tokyo Toronto Warsaw

and associated companies in
Berlin Ibadan

Oxford and *Oxford English*
are trade marks of Oxford University Press

ISBN 0 19 431414 6 (with answers)

First published 1995
Sixth impression 2000

Illustrated by Belinda Evans

Typeset in Wyvern Typesetting Ltd., Bristol

Printed in Hong Kong

For Sara and Joe

Introduction

Grammar Spectrum 3 is for intermediate students of English. It explains and practises the grammar that intermediate students need to learn. It can be used for self-study, for homework, and in class. This book is part of the *Grammar Spectrum* series of books; students can use the whole series to progress from an elementary to an intermediate level of English.

Using the book

When you have a particular grammar problem, you can look it up in the Contents at the front of the book, or in the Index at the back. You can then study the unit that deals with that problem. Or, you can work through the book from beginning to end.

Each unit begins with an explanation of the grammar point, and then it has a number of exercises for students to practise the grammar they have read about. Students can write their answers in the book, or on a separate piece of paper. When you have finished the exercises, you can check your answers in the answer key at the back of the book (page 102).

Grammar and spelling tables at the back of this book (pages 94–97) give information on plural and uncountable nouns, Present Simple forms, **-ing** forms, past participles, etc.

Finishing the book

When you have finished studying the whole book, you can do the Exit tests on pages 98 to 101. In the Exit tests, every question tests something from a unit with the same number. If you make a mistake, for example in question 30, you can look back to unit 30 and study that unit again. The answers to the Exit tests are on page 117.

Enjoy your studies.

Contents

1 Present Simple (**I know**)

1 The Present Simple has two forms (e.g. **know**, **knows**). We use **do** and **does** to make negatives, questions, and short answers:

POSITIVE
I/you/we/they **know**.
He/she/it **knows**.

NEGATIVE
I/you/we/they **don't** ⎫
He/she/it **doesn't** ⎬ **know**.

QUESTIONS
Do I/you/we/they ⎫
Does he/she/it ⎬ **know?**

SHORT ANSWERS
Yes, ⎰ I/you/we/they **do**.
⎱ he/she/it **does**.
No, ⎰ I/you/we/they **don't**.
⎱ he/she/it **doesn't**.

(For more information on the forms of the Present Simple, see Table C, page 95.)

2 Note also:
▶ plural nouns:
*The girls **know**.*
*The boys **don't** know.*
▶ singular nouns:
*Sarah **knows** the answer.*
*Michael **doesn't** know the answer.*

▶ uncountable nouns (e.g. **ice**, **water**, **cotton**, **information**):
*Ice **floats** on water.*
(For more details on uncountable nouns, see Table B, page 94.)

3 We use the Present Simple to talk about facts:
*Heat **rises**.*
*Does glass **float** on water? ~ No, it **doesn't**.*
*Fiona **doesn't eat** meat.*

4 We use the Present Simple to talk about repeated actions (e.g. habits or routines):

*He always **gets** up at 8 o'clock.*

*Do you **cycle** to work? ~ Yes, I **do**.*

5 We use the Present Simple with expressions of frequency (e.g. **twice a week**, **often**):
*We watch TV **two** or **three times a week**.*
*Tom doesn't practise **every day**.*
Note that we put adverbs (e.g. **never**, **often**, **usually**) before the main verb (e.g. **go**, **visit**):
*I **never** go to bed after midnight.*
*Do you **often** visit your grandparents?*

....

Practice

A Write the correct Present Simple form of the verb in brackets ( ). Sometimes you do not need to change the verb.

0 Jane __reads__ (read) 'The Guardian' newspaper, but I __read__ (read) 'The Independent'.

1 Fred _____ (cycle) to work, but his wife _____ (go) by car.

2 Mark _____ (say) he _____ (do) a lot of fishing, but he never _____ (catch) anything.

3 Jeff _____ (buy) his food in small shops, but Jane _____ (do) all her shopping at the supermarket.

4 Diana _____ (like) Physics, Chemistry and Biology; she always _____ (get) good marks in her science exams.

5 Susan _____ (live) in Leeds, but she _____ (work) in Bradford.

6 I _____ (leave) work at 6 o'clock, but John _____ (finish) work at 5 o'clock.

7 Mary _____ (ride) her bike to school and her father _____ (carry) her books.

8 For breakfast, Ann _____ (eat) cereal with milk and then she _____ (have) some toast.

B **Make Present Simple questions and answers from the words in brackets. Sometimes no change is required.**

0 (the President of the U.S.A./live/in New York? ~ No, he/do/. /He/live/in Washington.)

Does the President of the U.S.A . live in New York? ~ _No, he doesn't. He lives in Washington._

1 (modern trains/use/coal? ~ No, they/do/. /They/use/electricity.)

_____ ~ _____

2 (the Queen/often/wear/a crown? ~ No, she/do/. /She/usually/wear/a hat.)

_____ ~ _____

3 (wine/come/from oranges? ~ No, it/do/. /It/come/from grapes.)

_____ ~ _____

4 (Sri Lanka/export/coffee? ~ No, it/do/. / It/export/tea.)

_____ ~ _____

5 (potatoes/grow/on bushes? ~ No, they/do/. / They/grow/in the ground.)

_____ ~ _____

C **Now, using the words from exercise B, write negative sentences.**

0 _The President of the USA doesn't live in New York._

1 _____

2 _____

3 _____

4 _____

5 _____

D **Use the words in brackets to make sentences that are true; sometimes you will need *doesn't* or *don't*.**

0 (The sun/rise/in the East)   _The sun rises in the East._

0 (The sun/rise/in the West)   _The sun doesn't rise in the West._

1 (Ice/float/on water)   _____

2 (Lions/live/in the Arctic)   _____

3 (Winter/come/after spring)   _____

4 (Austrians/speak/German)   _____

5 (Cotton/come/from sheep)   _____

E **Look at these notes about different people's habits.**

Ruth Clark:	jog – twice a week	smoke – no
Neil Peters:	cycle – every day	drink beer – never
Mary Thomas:	swim – every weekend	smoke – 15 cigarettes a day
Bill Brown:	play tennis – once a week	smoke – no
Susan West:	swim – twice a week	drink alcohol – no

Now write sentences about these people, as in the example.

0 Ruth _jogs twice a week. She doesn't smoke._

1 Neil _____

2 Mary _____

3 Bill _____

4 Susan _____

2 Present Continuous (**I'm eating**)

1 We make the Present Continuous with the present tense of **be** and the **-ing** form of a verb:

I	am/'m ⎫
You/we/they	are/'re ⎬ eating.
He/she/it	is/'s ⎭

We make negatives, questions, and short answers like this:

*Jim **isn't speaking** to me.*
*You **aren't listening**.*
*Is Mary **working** in the garden? ~ Yes, she **is**.*
*Are the others **helping** her? ~ No, they **aren't**.*

(For more information on **-ing** forms, see Table D, page 95.)

2 We use the Present Continuous for actions in progress at the time of speaking:

3 We use the Present Continuous for an action that has started, that has not finished, and that will continue in the future. The action is not in progress at the time of speaking, but we often say **at the moment**:

4 We use the Present Continuous for a temporary action or situation that is different from a person's normal habits:

A: *Can I speak to Ann, please?*
B: *No, she's not at work. She**'s doing** a course in Norwich **this week**.*

5 We use the Present Continuous to talk about changes and trends. This use often goes with **nowadays**, **these days** etc.

*The earth's climate **is getting** warmer.*
*These days, more and more people **are going** abroad for their holidays.*

6 We can use the Present Continuous with **always** to say that something happens too often:

*Tom **is always asking** stupid questions.*
*They**'re always phoning** me at home.*

....

Practice

A Look at the pictures. Complete the sentences, describing the pictures, using the Present Continuous of a verb in the box. Use *He/She/It/They*, as in the example.

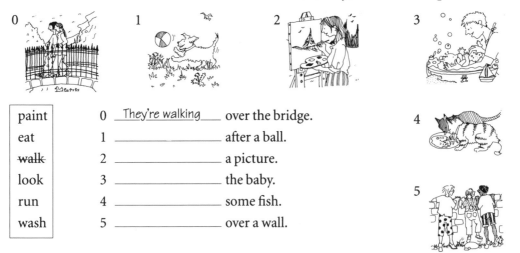

paint	0	_They're walking_ over the bridge.
eat	1	_____ after a ball.
~~walk~~	2	_____ a picture.
look	3	_____ the baby.
run	4	_____ some fish.
wash	5	_____ over a wall.

B Choose the best phrase from the box to complete these sentences. Put the verb in the Present Continuous.

> (sleep) in the sitting-room at the moment
> (do) a computer course this week
> ~~(not sleep) very well at the moment~~
> (go) to work by bus this week

0 A: You look tired.

B: Yes, I*'m not sleeping very well at the moment.*

1 A: Does Tim Sharp work with you?

B: Yes, but he's not here. He _____

2 My brother has borrowed my car. That's why I _____

3 The ceiling in our bedroom fell down so we _____

C What do people say about our world these days? Write complete sentences. Use the Present Continuous.

0 (The air/become/more polluted every year)

The air is becoming more polluted every year.

1 (Fashions/change/all the time these days)

_____

2 (More women/study/at university these days)

_____

3 (House prices/go/up all the time nowadays)

_____

4 (The sea/get/dirtier every year)

_____

D Use the words in brackets ( ) to complete these dialogues. Use the Present Continuous.

0 A: Why don't you like Adam?

B: (Because he/always/tell/stupid stories)

Because he's always telling stupid stories.

1 A: Why are you annoyed with Mary?

B: (Because she /always/ask/me for money)

_____

2 A: Why don't you like Pam and Paul?

B: (Because they/always/argue)

_____

3 A: Why are you annoyed with Susan?

B: (Because she/always/borrow/my CDs)

_____

4 A: Why don't you like Tom?

B: (Because he /always/ phone/me late at night)

_____

3 Present Simple (**I work**) or Present Continuous (**I'm working**)

Compare the Present Simple and the Present Continuous:

	Present Simple	**Present Continuous**
1	We use the Present Simple for things that are true at any time. We use it for a general truth, or a fact: *Things **fall** to the ground because of gravity. Ann **doesn't play** the violin very well, but she **plays** the piano beautifully.*	We use the Present Continuous to say that an action is in progress now, at the time we speak: *Look! The leaves **are falling** from the trees. Listen! Ann**'s playing** the piano; she**'s playing** something by Beethoven.*
2	We use the Present Simple when we talk about a permanent situation, or an activity that is repeated again and again. We think that it will continue for an unlimited time: *What **does** Fred **do**? ~ Fred's a journalist; he **writes** for a geographical magazine. I **work** for a company that **makes** computers. We **sell** them all over the world. Mary usually **studies** in the library. I **stay** with friends when I **go** on business trips to Japan.*	We use the Present Continuous to describe a current activity or situation that is unusual or temporary. We know it will continue for a limited period of time from now: *Fred **is writing** four articles about Africa. He did two yesterday. He'll do the rest tomorrow. I don't usually work at the weekends, but I**'m working** on Saturdays at the moment. Mary**'s studying** at home. The library is shut. Sue and Martin **are staying** in a friend's flat until they find a flat of their own.*
3	We use the Present Simple with words like **always, usually, often** etc. when we talk about how often we do something: *Mary **sometimes** studies at home, but she **usually** works in the library.*	We can use the Present Continuous with **always** to say that something happens too often: *Tom is **always** asking stupid questions. They**'re always** complaining.*

Practice

A   Look at this table.

Name	Home	Job	Current project	Project location
Mike	Glasgow	engineer	bridge design	Aberdeen
Sally	London	conference organiser	congress	Dublin
Philip	Leeds	salesman	trade fair	Birmingham
Jenny	Brighton	accountant	head office	London

Use these verbs in the Present Simple or the Present Continuous: *live, work, stay.*

0   Mike __lives__ in Glasgow and he __works__ as an engineer.

0   At the moment Mike __is staying__ in Aberdeen because he __is working__ on a bridge design there.

1   Sally _____ in London where she _____ as a conference organiser.

2   At the moment Philip _____ in Birmingham because he _____ at a trade fair there.

3 At the moment Sally _____ in Dublin because she _____ at a congress there.

4 Jenny _____ in Brighton where she _____ as an accountant.

5 Philip _____ in Leeds where he _____ as a salesman.

6 At the moment Jenny _____ in London because she _____ at head office.

B **Use the words in brackets ( ) to complete the dialogues. Use the Present Continuous or the Present Simple.**

0 (The sun/rise/in the east.)   0 (Look! The sun/come/up.)

   The sun rises in the east.   Look! The sun is coming up.

1 Ann: Is the swimming pool open today?

   Jane: (No, they/get/things ready for the next competition.)

   _____

   Ann: (How often/they/have/these competitions?)

   _____

   Jane: About three times a year.

2 Sam: (Why/that machine/not/work/at the moment?)

   _____

   Chris: (I don't know, but a mechanic/mend/it.)

   _____

   Sam: (What/the machine/do/in fact?) (it/make/boxes?)

   _____

   Chris: (Yes, it/make/boxes of all sizes.)

   _____

3 Mary: (Look! The Fosters/work/in their garden.)

   _____

   (They/not/usually/work/on Sundays.)

   _____

   Let's have a word with them. Hello, Joe. Hello, Sara. (you/get/ready/for the winter?)

   _____

   Joe: (Yes, we/tidy /up the leaves.)

   _____

   (We/always/try/to do it before the winter/come/.)

   _____

4 Tim: (Sam, what/you/look/for?)

   _____

   Sam: (I/look/for Jean's glasses.)

   _____

   (She/not/often/wear/them.)

   _____

   (She only/wear/them to read, so she often/lose/them.)

   _____

4 Verbs not used in continuous tenses

1 Look at this:

A: *What does Tom do?*
B: *He **sings** in a pop group.*

A: *What is Tom doing?*
B: *He**'s singing** with his band.*

Action verbs, like **sing**, are used in simple forms (e.g. **he sings**) and in continuous forms (e.g. **he's singing**). Most verbs (e.g. **sing, teach, study, talk, listen, sit, play** etc.) are verbs of action.

But some verbs do not describe actions. Look at this:

*Tom **has** a motorbike.*

*Tom **likes** Mary.*

Non-action verbs, like **have** (= 'possess'), **like, know**, are not usually used in continuous tenses:

Not ~~Tom is having a motorbike.~~
Not ~~Tom is liking Mary.~~

2 Non-action verbs include:

▶ verbs of thinking:

know	forget	notice
remember	recognize	understand

I know the answer. (Not ~~knowing the answer.~~)

▶ verbs of feeling:

hate	like	love	want

He likes ice-cream. (Not ~~He's liking…~~)

▶ other verbs:

be	cost	fit	hear
include	mean	need	own
matter	prefer	smell	sound

These shoes cost £55. (Not ~~…are costing…~~)

3 Some verbs have two meanings: one that describes an action, and one that does not:

look: *He's **looking** at the picture.* (action)
*He **looks** (= seems) tired.* (not an action)

taste: *John **is tasting** the soup.* (action)
*The soup **tastes** nice.* (not an action)

feel: *She**'s feeling** the material.*
*I **feel** (= am) cross about the accident.*

have: *What's she doing? She**'s having** lunch.*
*What's wrong? I **have** a headache.*

think: *Please be quiet. I**'m thinking**.*
*I **think** you're right.*

....

Practice

A Complete this text about a party. Put in the right words from the box in the right form, Present Simple (*I eat*) or Present Continuous (*I'm eating*). Use each verb once.

listen	like	sit	~~talk~~	want
drink	play	understand	think	

Everybody ⁰ *is talking*_____ very loudly. Tom ¹_____ near the CD player because he ²_____ to the music. 'Who ³_____ the guitar?' Judy asks him. 'It's Eric Clapton. I ⁴_____ he's fantastic,' says Tom. 'I ⁵_____ the music, but I don't ⁶_____ the words very well,' Judy says. At the end of the song, Judy says, 'Are you thirsty, Tom? ⁷____ you _____ a drink?' 'Yes, a glass of orange juice, please,' says Tom, 'I never ⁸_____ beer or wine.'

B Put in the words in the Present Simple or the Present Continuous. Sometimes you do not need to change the verb in brackets.

0 I _don't understand_ (not/understand) that sign over there. What _does it mean_ (it /mean)?

1 Paula and Jack are in the sitting-room. They _____ (listen) to the news, and Paula _____ (look) at a magazine as well.

2 The students _____ (count) the books in the library today, because we _____ (not/ know) how many we have.

3 Tim _____ (like) his new shoes; they _____ (fit) him perfectly.

4 June: Look! That woman _____ (sit) in your chair.
   Barry: It _____ (not/matter). I can sit over there.

5 This computer is very expensive. It _____ (cost) more than £3000, but the price _____ (include) tax.

C Use the Present Simple or the Present Continuous. Sometimes you do not need to change the verb.

0 Alan: (You/wear/your overcoat./you/go/out?)
           You're wearing your overcoat. Are you going out?

   Jane: (Yes,/I/go/the shops. I/need/some more paint.)
           Yes, I'm going to the shops. I need some more paint.

1 Adam: (you/recognize/the woman in this photo?)
           _____

   Susan: (you/mean/ the woman who/look/straight at the camera?)
           _____

2 Mark: (Hello, David. Why/you/stand/here?/you/wait/for me?)
           _____

   David: (Yes, I/want/to speak to you.)
           _____

3 James: (Listen to the engine. /you/think/it is all right?)
           _____

   Fiona: (It/sound/all right, but it/smell/of oil.)
           _____

D Complete each sentence using the words in the box.

| tastes | is tasting | feels | is feeling |
| has | is having | thinks | is thinking |

0 A customer _is feeling_ some curtain material.
1 She's smiling because she _____ about her boyfriend.
2 John is very rich. He _____ a house, a flat, and two cars.
3 The cook _____ the soup now .
4 This material _____ very soft.
5 This cake _____ delicious.
6 Sue _____ breakfast at the moment.
7 Pamela _____ English is an easy language to learn.

5 Past Simple (**I walked**)

1 We form the Past Simple like this:

> POSITIVE
> I/you/he/she/it/we/they **walked.**
>
> NEGATIVE
> I/you/he/she/it/we/they **didn't walk.**
>
> QUESTIONS
> **Did** I/you/he/she/it/we/they **walk?**
>
> SHORT ANSWERS
> Yes, I/you/he/she/it/we/they **did.**
> No, I/you/he/she/it/we/they **didn't.**

(For information on how to form Past Simple verbs, see Tables E and F on page 96.)

2 We use the Past Simple for single complete events in past time. We often use it with time expressions like **at 4 o'clock**, **yesterday**, **when?**, **in 1993** etc:

A: *When **did** you **win** the cup?*
B: *We **won** the cup **in 1993**.*
*We **went** to a concert **yesterday**.*

3 We use the Past Simple for complete events, even when they continued for a long time:
> A: *How long **did** the First World War **last**?*
> B: *It **lasted** for about 5 years, I think.*
> *My parents **lived** in Japan for three years. Then they went to live in Australia.*

4 We also use the Past Simple to talk about repeated events, or habits in the past:

*When George was young, he always **walked** to school.*

5 We use the Past Simple to tell a story in past time:
> *We **left** home early on Saturday morning and **drove**, without stopping, to the Scottish border. It **took** about 6 hours to get there. After we crossed the border, we **stopped** in a little village, and **had** something to eat…*

....

Practice

A Use the words in brackets ( ) to make a question and an answer. Use the Past Simple.

0 (When/Kennedy/die?)   ~ (He/in 1963)
   When did Kennedy die?   ~ He died in 1963.

1 (What/Marie Curie/discover/in 1898?)   ~ (She /radium)
   _____   ~ _____

2 (Where/Michelangelo/live?)   ~ (He /in Florence)
   _____   ~ _____

3 (When/Margaret Thatcher/become/Prime Minister?) ~ (She/Prime Minister in 1979)
   _____   ~ _____

4 (What/Alexander Bell/invent?)   ~ (He /the telephone)
   _____   ~ _____

5 (How many books/Agatha Christie/write?)   ~ (She /over a hundred books)
   _____   ~ _____

6 (When/Greta Garbo/move/to the United States.) ~ (She /there in 1925)
   _____   ~ _____

B In each case the two facts were true many years ago. Write a sentence to describe the past situation, as in the example.

0 (It is 1984.) Sally is at school. She plays in a football team.
   When _Sally was at school, she played in a football team_

1 (It is 1987.) Bob's sister is at university. She writes a lot of poetry.
   When _____

2 (It is 1990.) Fred is in the army. He goes to many different countries.
   When _____

3 (It is 1992.) Jane and Michael are at school. They don't do much homework.
   When _____

4 (It is 1985.) Anna is a teenager. She wears very long skirts.
   When _____

C Put the right form of the best verb from the box in each sentence. Use each verb once. Then write the sentences in the correct order so they tell a story.

| be | believe | decide | eat | enjoy | get | talk |
| go | last | ~~leave~~ | make | see | ~~take~~ | tell |

After I __left__ school, I __took__ a job on the railways.

We _____ by train, of course.

In particular, we _____ some mushrooms that _____ as big as plates.

We _____ everyone about the size of the mushrooms when we _____ back home.

But nobody _____ us.

Of course, we _____ all the famous buildings in Rome. They were fascinating.

We _____ to go together to Rome.

I _____ friends with a man called Harry.

But most of all, we _____ the delicious Italian food.

Sometimes, we _____ about our ideas for a holiday.

The journey _____ over 24 hours.

0 _After I left school, I took a job on the railways._
1 _____
2 _____
3 _____
4 _____
5 _____
6 _____
7 _____
8 _____
9 _____
10 _____

6 Past Simple (**I waited**) or Past Continuous (**I was waiting**)

Compare the Past Simple and the Past Continuous:

Past Simple	Past Continuous

1

I/you/he/she/it/we/they { **talked.** / **didn't talk.** }

Did I/you/he/she/it/we/they **talk?**

I/he/she/it **was/wasn't** } **talking.**
You/we/they **were/weren't** }

Was I/he/she/it } **talking?**
Were you/we/they }

2

We use the Past Simple to talk about a complete event in the past:

*Last Saturday morning, Paul **played** football in the park.*

past ———————————————→ (now)

| Paul played football. |

Here are some more examples:
*On Sunday I **made** a cake.*
*It **rained** a lot on Saturday morning.*

We use the Past Continuous to talk about an action that was in progress, when something else happened:

Last Saturday, Paul was playing football in the park when he saw Jane.

past ———————————————→ (now)

| Paul was playing football. |
| He saw Jane. |

Here are some more examples:
*The phone rang while I **was making** a cake.*
*It **was raining** when we left home.*

3

We often use the Past Simple to talk about one event that followed another event:

*When Ann James **left** university, she **went** to work for a bank. She **left** the bank after five years, and **wrote** a book which ...*

In a story we often use the Past Continuous to say what was in progress, when something happened:

*The sun **was shining**. People **were sitting** under the trees or **walking** around the park. Suddenly a car **drove** into the park ...*

Practice

A **Use the Past Simple and the Past Continuous to make sentences from the words in brackets.**

0 (The police/arrive/while/I/have/breakfast)
    The police arrived while I was having breakfast.

1 (The storm/start/while/they/drive/home)
_____

2 (I/see/an accident/while /I/wait/for the bus)
_____

3 (Mary/go/to several concerts/while/she/stay/in London)
_____

0 (I/have/breakfast/when/the police/arrive)
    I was having breakfast when the police arrived.

4 (My father/cook/the dinner /when /he/burn/his fingers)
_____

5 (The soldiers/prepare/to leave/when/the bomb/explode)
_____

B Complete these texts using the Past Simple or the Past Continuous of the verbs in brackets.

0 Beethoven _wrote_ (write) nine symphonies; he _was writing_ (write) another symphony when he died.

1 Last Saturday Tom wanted to make two salads. He _____ (make) the first one in five minutes. He _____ (make) the second one when his guests _____ (arrive), and they _____ (help) him to finish it.

2 The artist Gaudi _____ (design) several houses in Barcelona, Spain. Later he _____ (start) work on a church. He _____ (work) on the church when he _____ (die).

3 Last month a bank robber _____ (escape) while the police _____ (take) him to prison. Later they _____ (catch) him again, and this time they _____ (lock) him up without any problem.

4 Philip's football team were lucky last Saturday. After 20 minutes they _____ (lose), but in the end they _____ (win) the game by 4 goals to 2.

5 John Lennon _____ (sing) and _____ (play) on many records with the Beatles. After that he _____ (record) several songs without the Beatles. He _____ (prepare) a new record when Mark Chapman _____ (shoot) him.

6 The evening was getting darker; the street lights _____ (come) on. People _____ (hurry) home after work. I _____ (stand) in a queue at the bus stop. Suddenly somebody _____ (grab) my bag.

C A policewoman is interviewing Mary Croft about last Friday evening. Look at the pictures and complete the conversation. Use the Past Simple or the Past Continuous of the words in brackets.

Policewoman:	What time 0 _did you get_ (you/get) home from work?
Mary:	At about 6 o'clock.
Policewoman:	And what 1_____ (you /do) after you got home?
Mary:	I read the newspaper.
Policewoman:	Did anything happen while 2_____ (read) the paper?
Mary:	Yes, the phone 3_____ (ring) .
Policewoman:	What 4_____ (you/do) when your husband came home?
Mary:	I was watching TV, and I 5_____ (drink) a cup of coffee.
Policewoman:	Did you and your husband stay at home?
Mary:	No, I 6_____ (drink) my coffee. Then I put on my raincoat, and we 7_____ (go) out at seven o'clock.
Policewoman:	Why 8_____ (you/put) your raincoat on?
Mary:	Because it 9_____ (rain), of course.

7 Present Simple, Past Simple, and **used to** (**I used to know**)

1 We can use the Present Simple to talk about present situations or habits:
- ▶ situations:
  *My sister **works** as a translator.*
  *Andrew **lives** in London.*
- ▶ habits:
  *Peter usually **wears** jeans.*
  *I often **eat** a sandwich for lunch.*
  *Mike **doesn't smoke** any more.*
  ***Does** John **drive** to work every day?*

2 Look at these sentences with the Past Simple:
- ▶ situation:
  *Henry **lived** in France for many years.*
- ▶ habit:
  *When I was young, I **ran** three miles every day.*

The verbs are in the Past Simple and the sentences are about past situations or habits.

3 Look at these sentences with **used to**:
  *Jill **used to live** in Ireland.*
  *Many people **used to make** their own bread.*
  *My husband **used to work** at home.*

We use **used to** to talk about a past situation or habit that continued for months or years, and to emphasize that the situation today is different:
  *Jill doesn't live in Ireland **now**.*
  ***Nowadays** people usually buy bread from a shop.*
  *My husband doesn't work at home **now**.*

Compare the Past Simple and **used to**:
- ▶ Past Simple: *When he was young, he **ran** three miles every day.* (He may or may not run 3 miles every day now.)
- ▶ **used to**: *When I was young, I **used to run** three miles every day. I don't do that now.* (I don't run 3 miles everyday now.)

We make negative sentences and questions with **did + use to** :
  *Sue **didn't use to like** black coffee.*
  *Paul **didn't use to smoke** a pipe.*
  ***Did** Alan **use to cycle** to school?*
  ***Did** your parents **use to read** to you?*

4 We do not use **use to** for present situations or habits; we use the Present Simple:
  *Ann **sings** in a band.*
  (Not ~~Ann uses to sing in a band.~~)
  *Joe **doesn't cycle** to school.*
  (Not ~~…doesn't use to cycle…~~)

....

Practice

A **Use the words in brackets ( ) to make complete sentences. Use a Past Simple and a Present Simple verb in each sentence.**

0 (Yesterday Ian/get/up at 7.15, but he normally/get/up at 8)

  <u>Yesterday Ian got up at 7.15, but he normally gets up at 8.</u>

0 (Fred usually/walk/to work , but last week he/go/by car)

  <u>Fred usually walks to work, but last week he went by car.</u>

1 (Last Sunday Mike/stay/at home, but he normally/go/fishing)

  _____

2 (We usually/swim/in the sea, but last Sunday we/swim /in the river)

  _____

3 (Last summer, Bob/have/a short holiday, but he usually/have/a long holiday)

  _____

4 (Mrs Jones normally/sleep/for seven hours every night, but last night she/sleep/for nine hours)

  _____

5 (I usually/enjoy/the food in this restaurant, but I/not/like /it yesterday)

  _____

6 (Peter/usually/do/his homework, but he /not /do /it yesterday)

_____

B Complete the questions. Use the Present Simple or the Past Simple.

0 Sally: My sister and I usually work on Saturdays.

Tim: <u>Did</u> you <u>work</u> last Saturday as well?

0 Robin: Last Sunday Peter went to bed at 9 o'clock.

Diana: <u>Does</u> he usually <u>go</u> to bed at 9 o'clock?

1 Jeff: Neil had a cold shower yesterday.

Helen: _____ he usually _____ a cold shower?

2 Kate: Bob wakes up very early almost every day.

John: _____ he _____ very early yesterday as well?

3 Mary: My cousins usually send us a card at Christmas.

Jim: _____ they _____ you a card last Christmas?

4 Susan: Paula phoned me again last night.

Derek: _____ she often _____ you?

C Look at this table of people who have changed what they eat or drink.

name	in the past	now
Ann	meat	fish
Tom	coffee	tea
Robert	white bread	brown bread
Pam	tap water	bottled water
Mary	tinned fruit	fresh fruit
Susan	margarine	butter

Now make sentences, as in the examples.

0 Ann <u>used to eat</u> meat, but now <u>she eats</u> fish.

0 Tom <u>drinks tea</u> now, but <u>he used to drink</u> coffee.

1 Robert _____ white bread, but now _____ brown bread.

2 Pam _____ tap water, but now _____ bottled water.

3 Mary _____ fresh fruit now, but _____ tinned fruit.

4 Susan _____ butter now, but _____ margarine.

Now complete these questions.

0 <u>Did Ann use to eat</u> meat? ~ Yes she did, but now she eats fish.

5 _____ white bread? ~ Yes he did, but now he eats brown bread.

6 _____ tinned fruit? ~ Yes she did, but now she eats fresh fruit.

7 _____ tap water? ~ Yes she did, but now she drinks bottled water.

Now complete these sentences.

0 Ann <u>didn't use to eat</u> fish, but she does now.

0 Tom drinks tea now, but he <u>didn't use to drink</u> it.

8 Susan _____ butter, but she does now.

9 Mary eats fresh fruit now, but she _____ it.

10 Pam drinks bottled water now, but she _____ it.

8 Present Perfect (**I have eaten**)

1 We make the Present Perfect with **have** or **has** and a past participle (e.g. **walked**, **taken**):

I/you/we/they	**have/'ve** ⎫
He/she/it	**has/'s** ⎭ **started.**

We make negatives, questions, and short answers with **have** or **has**:
> You **haven't started.**
> Diana **hasn't started.**
> **Have** you **started?** ~ Yes, I **have.**
> **Has** Diana **started?** ~ No, she **hasn't.**

2 With regular verbs, we add -**ed** to form the past participle (e.g. **walked**, **started**). But there are many verbs with irregular past participles (e.g. **taken**, **chosen**, **sold**, **slept**). For more details on past participle forms, see Tables E and F on page 96.

3 We use the Present Perfect to talk about events in past time, but not about when they happened:
> Somebody has taken my bag.
> (Not Somebody has taken it yesterday.)
> I **have read** her latest novel.

We use the Present Perfect in this way when the past event is relevant now:
> Somebody **has taken** my bag. I can't find it.
> I**'ve been** to the dentist. My tooth doesn't hurt now.

4 We use the Present Perfect to talk about situations or actions during a period that started in the past, and has continued up to the present (e.g. **today**, **this month**, **this year**, **for three weeks**, **since last year**):
> We**'ve lived** here **for six years.**
>   (= from six years ago until now)
> I**'ve worked** at CGE **since 1992.**
>   (= from 1992 until now)
> Jane **has phoned** me three times **this week.**
> We **haven't saved** much money **this year.**
> **Have** you **seen** Neil (**today**)?

5 We can use the Present Perfect with **ever**, **never**, **already**, and **yet**, like this:
> **Have** you **ever been** inside a submarine?
> I**'ve never eaten** horse meat.
> Chris **has already sent** her a present.
> They **haven't finished** their game **yet.**

Note that we put **ever**, **never** and **already** before the past participle, and **yet** at the end of the sentence.

....

Practice

A **Use the words in brackets ( ) to make questions and answers with the Present Perfect.**

0 (have/you/eat/anything?)   ~ (Yes, I/have/eat/a lot.)
  <u>Have you eaten anything?</u>   ~   <u>Yes, I've eaten a lot.</u>

1 (have/Tom/buy/anything?)   ~ (Yes, he/have/buy/a new suit.)
  _____ ~ _____

2 (have/Jane/give/him any money?)   ~ (Yes, she/have/give/him £10.)
  _____ ~ _____

3 (have/you/break/anything?)   ~ (Yes, I/have/break/a plate.)
  _____ ~ _____

4 (have/Pam/choose/a present?)   ~ (Yes, she/have/choose/this novel.)
  _____ ~ _____

5 (have/they/bring/any food?)   ~ (Yes, they/have/bring/some sandwiches.)
  _____ ~ _____

B   Say what has happened in each situation. Use the words in brackets and the Present Perfect.

0   Your bike is not where you left it.
(somebody/take/my bike)   _Somebody has taken my bike._

1   The garage door was closed; now it is open.
(somebody/open/the garage door) _____

2   There are no biscuits in the cupboard.
(somebody/eat/all the biscuits) _____

3   The kitchen window was all right; now it is smashed.
(somebody/break/the kitchen window) _____

4   Mary's watch is not where she left it.
(somebody/steal/Mary's watch) _____

5   Your orange juice was in the fridge; it isn't there now.
(somebody/drink/my orange juice) _____

6   Your shoes are not where you left them.
(somebody/take/my shoes) _____

C   An inventor wants to advertise a new product. This week, he must send out a letter and organize a newspaper advertisement. He has made a list of jobs, and he has ticked (✓) the things he has already done.

0	prepare the circular letter ✓	2	put the copies in the envelopes
0	buy the stamps	3	write the text of the advertisement ✓
1	make copies of the letter ✓	4	send the advertisement to the paper

Write positive sentences with *already*, and negative sentences with *yet*.

0   _He has already prepared the circular letter._

0   _He hasn't bought the stamps yet._

1   _____

2   _____

3   _____

4   _____

D   Make complete questions and answers from the words in brackets.

0   (have/you/see/Kate this week?   ~ No, I/have/not/see/her since last month)
Have you seen Kate this week?   ~   _No, I haven't seen her since last month._

1   (have/Sue/win/any tennis competitions this year? ~ Yes, she/have/ win/three this year)
_____   ~   _____

2   (have/you/shave/today?   ~ No, I/have/not/shave/since yesterday)
_____   ~   _____

3   (have/you/sell/many TVs this month?   ~ Yes, we/have/sell/23 this month)
_____   ~   _____

4   (have/you/play/tennis this week?   ~ No, I/have/not/play/for a month)
_____   ~   _____

9 Past Simple (**I ate**) or Present Perfect (**I have eaten**)(1)

1 We can use the Past Simple, but not the Present Perfect, to ask questions with **What time?**, **When?** etc, and to make statements about when things happened (e.g. **at 5 o'clock, in 1977**):

A: *What time* **did** *the plane* **land**?
(Not *What time has the plane landed?*)
B: *It* **landed** *at 5 o'clock.*
(Not *It has landed at 5 o'clock.*)

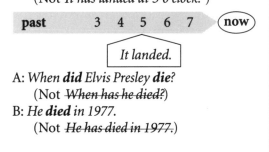

A: *When* **did** *Elvis Presley* **die**?
(Not *When has he died?*)
B: *He* **died** *in 1977.*
(Not *He has died in 1977.*)

2 We also use the Past Simple if other expressions set the event in past time:

When I was in the army, I **had** *a terrible time.*
(Not *I've had…*)
I **was** *almost back home when the storm started.*

3 We describe a past action or event with the Present Perfect to show that it is relevant now. The time of the action is not important.

Ann **has broken** *her arm.*
(= It is now broken.)
Bill **has made** *the salad.*
(= The salad is now made.)
The Past Simple does not imply anything about the situation now:
James **broke** *his arm last year.*
Kate **broke** *her arm yesterday.*
From this information we expect, of course, that James's arm is all right now, but that Kate's arm is still broken.

4 We introduce an event with the Present Perfect, but we continue to talk about it with the Past Simple:

A: *Ann's* **broken** *her arm.*
B: *How* **did** *she* **break** *it?*
A: *She* **fell** *onto some rocks.*

5 For a very recent event we can use the Present Perfect with **just** or the Past Simple with **ago**:

John **has just gone** *out.*
John **went** *out a few minutes* **ago**.
Note that we use **just** before the past participle (e.g. **gone**).

....

Practice

A Complete the sentences with the correct form of a verb from the box.

| die   go   ~~write~~   marry   paint   win |

0   Bob Dylan _wrote_____ 'Blowin' in the Wind' in 1962.
1   Mark Spitz _____ seven Olympic gold medals in 1972.
2   Pablo Picasso _____ 'Guernica' in 1937.
3   Marlene Dietrich _____ to Hollywood in 1930.
4   Louis Armstrong _____ in 1971.
5   Diana _____ Prince Charles in 1981.

B Use the words in brackets ( ) to complete the sentences.

0   When I was at school, (I/not/like/history) _I didn't like history._____
0   (My mother/be/at work) _My mother was at work_____ when the explosion happened.
1   (I/meet/Brian) _____ when we were in the army.
2   (I/be/in the garden) _____ when you phoned.
3   When Sam was young, (she/love/swimming) _____

4   (I/buy/these shoes) _____ when I was paid last week.

` 5   When Neil was sixteen, (he/have/very long hair) _____

6   When he saw her, (he/smile) _____

C   **If the first sentence is true, do we know that the second sentence is true? Write *Yes* or *Don't know*.**

0	John grew a beard.	John has a beard now.	Don't know.
0	Bob has grown a moustache.	Bob has a moustache now.	Yes.
1	Ruth went to Italy.	Ruth is in Italy now.	_____
2	Sarah has opened the door.	The door is now open.	_____
3	Ian has gone abroad.	Ian is abroad now.	_____
4	Bill opened the windows.	The windows are open now.	_____

D   **Complete these dialogues using the words in brackets. Use the Present Perfect or the Past Simple.**

0   A: Why are you crying?

B: Look. (I/cut/my hand) _I've cut my hand._____

A: (How/it/happen?) _How did it happen?_____

1   A: Is that a telegram?

B: Yes. It says that (Jane/have/a baby boy) _____

A: (When/she/have/the baby?) _____

2   A: Why are you looking so cross, Jeff?

B: Look. (Mary/break/my camera) _____

A: (How/she/break/it?) _____

3   A: What's the problem, Jason?

B: Look. (My bicycle/disappear) _____

A: (Where/you/leave/it?) _____

4   A: What's the matter with Paul?

B: (He/lose/his bag.) _____

A: (When/he/lose/it?) _____

5   A: What's that piece of paper?

B: It's my certificate. (I/pass/my exam) _____

A: (What mark/you/get?) _____

E   **Express these sentences in a different way. Use *just* or *a few minutes ago*.**

0   Mary has just phoned. _Mary phoned a few minutes ago._____

1   Kathy came home a few minutes ago. _____

2   Colin has just finished his lunch. _____

3   Michael has just had a shower. _____

4   Jenny went to bed a few minutes ago. _____

10 Past Simple or Present Perfect (2); **ago**, **for**, **since**

Compare the Past Simple and the Present Perfect:

Past Simple	Present Perfect

1 Look at this example of the Past Simple:
*There **were** many earthquakes **last century**.*
 	
past ⟶ (now)
     | *last century* |
 	
Note that **last century** is a period of past time. It ended before now.
	Look at this example of the Present Perfect:
	*There **have been** many earthquakes **this century**.*
	
	past ⟶ (now)
	           | *this century* |
	
	Note that **this century** is a period of time that includes now (the time of speaking).

2 We use the Past Simple to talk about events or situations in a period of past time:
  A: *How long **did** you **work in your last job**?*
  B: *I **worked** there for **four years**.*
 	
Did you **go** to the cinema **last week**?*
*Sheila **did not go** to work **yesterday**.*
We use the Past Simple for events in the lifetime of someone who is dead:
  A: ***Did** your grandmother ever **visit** Canada?*
  B: *Yes, she **spent** several holidays there.*
	We use the Present Perfect for events or situations in a period of time that includes now:
	  A: *How long **have** you **worked** here?*
	  B: *I've **worked** here **since last summer**.*
	   (I still work here.)
	
	Have you **been** to the cinema **this week**?*
	*Sheila **has not gone** to work **today**.*
	We use the Present Perfect for events in the lifetime of a living person:
	  A: ***Have** you ever **visited** Canada?*
	  B: *Yes, I've **had** several holidays there.*

3 Notice how a sentence with the Past Simple and one with the Present Perfect can give similar information from different points of view. Notice the use of **ago**, **for** and **since**:

*Pam **went** to live in Dublin **5 years ago**.*	*Pam **has lived** in Dublin **for five years**.* *Pam **has lived** in Dublin **since her wedding**.* *(or ... **since she got married**.)*

(For more details about **ago**, **for** and **since**, see unit 41.)

....

Practice

A **Complete the sentences with the Past Simple or the Present Perfect of the verb in brackets.**

0 (be) There __were__ a lot of accidents last year, and there __have been__ a lot this year, too.

0 (see) I __have__ not __seen__ Jane today, but I __saw__ her yesterday.

1 (win) Our team is very good. We _____ two competitions last year, and we _____ two this year as well.

2 (make) The factory _____ more than 1,000 motorbikes this year; it _____ not _____ so many last year.

3 (be) I'm worried about Mary. She _____ ill last week, and she _____ ill most of this week as well.

4 (work) Joe _____ not _____ hard last month, but he _____ hard this month.

5 (earn) I _____ a lot of money this year - much more than I _____ last year.

6 (rain) It _____ not _____ much last year here, and it _____ not _____ much this year, either.

B **In the brackets, the first year is when the person was born. If there is a second year, it is when the person died. Put the verbs into the Past Simple or the Present Perfect.**

0 Susan Cowley (1947–) is an artist. She _has painted_ (paint) in many different styles and she _has had_ (have) exhibitions in 14 countries.

1 Timothy Spinks (1846–1927) was a biologist. He _____ (study) the plants of New Zealand, and he _____ (write) several books on biology.

2 Claire Fox (1957–) is a doctor. She _____ (develop) new treatments for several diseases, and she _____ (make) several TV programmes about medicine.

3 Catherine Knight (1824–1883) was a nurse. She _____ (work) mainly with soldiers, and she _____ (spend) most of her life trying to improve their lives.

4 Steven Brock (1963–) is a golf player. He _____ (win) several competitions, and he _____ (earn) a lot of money from advertising different products.

C **Use the words in brackets to express the same information from a different point of view. Use the Present Perfect or the Past Simple.**

0 Ben stopped smoking five years ago.
(not/smoke/for) _Ben hasn't smoked for five years._

0 Jane has lived in Bristol for two years.
(move/to/ago) _Jane moved to Bristol two years ago._

1 Anna and John moved to London after their wedding.
(live/in/since) _____

2 Mary started working in France 6 months ago.
(work/for) _____

3 Pam stopped playing tennis when she was 15.
(not/play/since) _____

4 Fred hasn't eaten meat for 2 years.
(stop/eating/ago) _____

D **Summary exercise: study units 9 and 10, before you do this exercise.**
Use the words in brackets, and put them in the gaps in the Past Simple or the Present Perfect.

Policeman: Mr. Leach, how many times 0 _have you been_ (you/be) in prison?

Jim Leach: Twice.

Policeman: When 1_____ (you/finish) your last prison sentence?

Jim Leach: I 2_____ (come) out of prison about 6 months ago.

Policeman: How long 3_____ (you/live) in this town?

Jim Leach: About 7 years. I 4_____ (move) here when I got married.

Policeman: So you 5_____ (be) married for seven years.

Jim Leach: No, my wife 6_____ (leave) me two years ago.

Policeman: 7_____ (you/see) her since she left you?

Jim Leach: No, she 8_____ (phone) me a few days ago. I 9_____ (meet) her once about a year ago, but I 10_____ (not/see) her since then.

11 Present Perfect Simple (**I have done**) or Present Perfect Continuous (**I have been doing**)

Oct. 20/2008

Compare the Present Perfect Simple and Continuous:

	Present Perfect Simple	**Present Perfect Continuous**
1	I/you/we/they **have/'ve** He/she/it **has/'s** } eaten.	I/you/we/they **have/'ve** He/she/it **has/'s** } been eating.
2	We use the Present Perfect Simple (**have painted**) to talk about a past activity that is now completed: *We**'ve painted** the rooms.* (= The rooms are now painted.) *Anna**'s mended** her bike.* (= She can ride it now.)	We use the Present Perfect Continuous (**have been painting**) to emphasize the activity itself, which may or may not be completed: *We**'ve been painting** the flat. That's why it smells. We still have three rooms to paint.* *Anna's hands are dirty because she**'s been mending** her bike.*
3	We use the Present Perfect Simple to ask and answer **How many?, How much?**: A: *How many rooms **have** you **painted**?* B: *We**'ve painted** three of them.*	We usually use the Present Perfect Continuous to ask **How long?**, and with **since** and **for**: A: *How long **have** you **been waiting**? Have you **been queuing** for a long time?* B: *I**'ve been waiting** since 2 o'clock.*

4 Note that we usually use the Present Perfect Simple (not the Continuous):
  ▶ to talk about short actions with **have, stop, break**, etc:
    *Tony **has had** an accident on his bike.*
  ▶ with verbs of thinking (e.g. **know, decide, forget, notice**):
    *I'm sorry. I**'ve forgotten** your name.*
  ▶ to talk about the last time that something happened:
    *I **haven't eaten** meat for two years.* (= I last ate meat two years ago.)
Note that we can use the Present Perfect Simple or the Continuous with
work, teach, and **live**, with no difference in meaning:
    *I **have taught** here for two years.* or *I **have been teaching** here for two years.*

Practice

A Write out the sentences in brackets ( ). Use the Present Perfect Simple
(e.g. *I have done*).

0 He's late again. (How many times/he/arrive/late this month?)
    How many times has he arrived late this month?

1 What a good week! (We/sell/much more than we expected.)

    _____

2 (How much money/you/spend/this week?)

    _____

3 (How many people/Jane/invite/to her party?)

    _____

Now use the Present Perfect Continuous (*I have been doing*).

4   It's still raining. (It/rain/for hours.)

_____

5   That noise is awful. (They/drill/holes in the wall all morning.)

_____

6   Are you still here? (How long/you/sit/here?)

_____

B   **Five friends have just finished some jobs. Look at the table.**

	Activity	Now
Neil	sweep the floors	he is sweating
Rachel	cut the grass	she is tired
Paul	do the washing-up	he has soft hands
Carol	peel the onions	she has red eyes
Tim	defrost the fridge	he has cold hands

Complete the dialogues from this information. Use the Present Perfect Simple or Continuous.

0   Neil, why are you sweating? ~ Because I _have been sweeping the floors._

0   Is the lawn finished? ~ Yes, Rachel _has cut the grass._

1   Paul, why are your hands so soft? ~ Because I _____

2   Are the onions ready for the pan? ~ Yes, Carol _____ them.

3   Rachel, you look tired. ~ Yes, I _____

4   Tim, your hands are very cold. ~ Yes, I _____

5   Are the floors clean? ~ Yes, Neil _____ them.

6   Why are your eyes red, Carol? ~ Because I _____

7   Are the plates clean? ~ Yes, Paul _____

8   Is the fridge all right now? ~ Yes, Tim _____

C   **Put the verbs in brackets into the gaps in the right form. Use the Present Perfect Simple or Continuous.**

0   Ellen: Where are you and your family going to live?

    Ian: Well, we've _been talking_____ (talk) about that for weeks, but we

             haven't _decided_____ (decide) anything yet.

1   Tina: Excuse me. Have you _____ (stand) in this queue for a

             long time?

    Larry: Yes, I've _____ (queue) for almost an hour.

2   Sara: Why are you crying?

    Joe: Because my brother has _____ (have) an accident. He's

             _____ (break) both his legs.

3   Susan: Excuse me. Whose is this bag? Who has _____ (leave) it

             here?

    Wally: I don't know. I've _____ (sit) here all afternoon, but I

             haven't _____ (notice) it until now.

12 Past Perfect (**I had eaten**)

1 We form the Past Perfect with **had** and the past participle of a verb (e.g. **started**, **taken**):

| I/you/he/she/it/we/they | **had/'d** | **started**. |

*I **had taken** it.* or *I'**d taken** it.*
*They **had not started**.* or *They **hadn't** started**.*

2 Study this:

> A year ago:
>   Jenny is flying to Rome. She thinks, '*I have never been on a plane before now.*'
> Now:
>   *Jenny flew to Rome last year. She **had** never **been** on a plane before that.*

When we talk about an event or situation in past time we use the Past Simple (e.g. **flew**); if we talk about an event before that time, we use the Past Perfect (e.g. **had been**). Here is another example:

> Last Saturday at the cinema:
>   Mary: *We don't need to queue because I've already bought the tickets.*
> Now:
>   Mary: *We didn't need to queue because I **had** already **bought** the tickets.*

Note that we can use **never** and **already** before the past participle (e.g. **been**, **bought**).

3 If we talk about a series of past events in order, we use the Past Simple:
>   **A** *I saw a beautiful bird in my garden.* **B** *I went to get my camera.* **C** *The bird flew away.* **D** *I returned with my camera.*

> **past**   A B C D   (now)

We need the Past Perfect to make it clear that one of the events is not in order:
>   **D** *I returned with my camera.* **C** *The bird **had** already **flown** away.* (The bird had gone before I returned.)

Also, compare these sentences using **when**:

▶
Past Perfect: **When I returned with my camera, the bird had flown away.** (The bird went before I returned.)

▶
Past Simple: **When I returned with my camera, the bird flew away.** (The bird went after I returned.)

4 The Past Perfect is used in reported speech:
'*I have suffered from asthma for many years.*'
*She told the doctor that she **had suffered** from asthma for many years.*
(For more on reported speech, see unit 33.)

....

Practice

A Write sentences about what these people had already done or had never done before. Use the Past Perfect, and *already* or *never*.

0   Last summer Mary won a gold medal for the third time.
    She had already won two gold medals _____ before that.

0   Last year Ken visited Scotland for the first time.
    He had never visited Scotland _____ before that.

1   Last weekend Tom rode a horse for the first time.
    He _____ before that.

2   Last summer Jeff ran in a marathon for the sixth time.
    He _____ before that.

3   Last week Susan wrote a poem for the first time.
    She _____ before that.

4   Last week Ann appeared on TV for the first time.
    She _____ before that.

5   Last summer Tony played tennis at Wimbledon for the fifth time.
     He _____ before that.

6   Last year Jean wrote her third novel.
     She _____ before that.

B   **In each case you have two events in the order they took place. Write the information in one sentence using the words in brackets.**

0   **A** The driver started the car. **B** Lady James appeared.
     (When Lady James/appear/, the driver/already/start/the car)
     When Lady James appeared, the driver had already started the car.

1   **A** We put the fire out. **B** The firemen arrived.
     (When the firemen/arrive/, we/already/put/the fire out)
     _____

2   **A** Jim finished the work. **B** The manager came back.
     (When the manager/come/back, Jim/already/finish/the work)
     _____

3   **A** I went to bed. **B** Philip telephoned.
     (When Philip/telephone/, I/already/go/to bed)
     _____

4   **A** Alice and Jack had lunch. **B** Their children came home.
     (When their children/come/home, Alice and Jack/already/have/lunch)
     _____

5   **A** Ian prepared the supper. **B** His wife got home from work.
     (When his wife/get/home from work, Ian/already/prepare/the supper)
     _____

6   **A** The thieves spent the money. **B** The police caught them.
     (The thieves/already/spend/the money, when the police/catch/them)
     _____

C   **Use the Past Perfect to complete the sentences.**

0   Last summer Pam said, 'I've always wanted to fly in a helicopter.'
     Pam said that she _had always wanted to fly in a helicopter._

1   Fred said, 'Jack has just gone out.'
     Fred told us that Jack _____

2   Robert said to Jill, 'Have you been to Cambridge?'
     Robert asked Jill if she _____

3   When the boys came home, Mrs Brock said, 'I've made some sandwiches.'
     Mrs Brock told the boys that she _____

4   'I know your cousin,' said Tom. 'I met her in Amsterdam.'
     Tom said he knew my cousin because he _____

5   Bob was talking to Jean, and he said, 'Have you ever been to Japan?'
     Bob asked Jean if she _____

13 Future: **will**, **be going to**, Present Continuous and Simple

1 We can talk about future time with different verb forms, for example:
- ▶ **will**: *I'll come with you.*
- ▶ **be going to**: *He's going to come with us.*
- ▶ Present Continuous: *We're coming tomorrow.*

2 When we talk about events in the future that we expect to happen but that are not in our control, we can use **will** or **be going to**:

Ann **will be** (or **is going to be**) *12 next week.*

We **won't see** (or **aren't going to see**) *those birds again until next spring.*

Will *they* **finish** (or **Are** *they* **going to finish**) *the building soon?*

3 When we talk about events in the future that are in our control (i.e. we can decide what will happen), we use **will** differently from **be going to**. We use **will** at the time we decide what to do; we use **be going to** after we have decided what to do. Look at these examples:

John: *Can somebody help me, please?*
Helen: *Yes, I'll help you.*
(Here Brenda decided <u>after</u> John asked.)

Now compare:
Carol: *John needs some help.*
Helen: *I know. I'm going to help him.*
(Here Helen had decided <u>before</u> Carol spoke.)

4 Look at these examples:

If it rains, they'll stay (or *they're going to stay*) *at home.*

We'll have (or *we're going to have*) *lunch after the programme finishes.*

When a sentence has two parts that refer to the future, we use the Present Simple after **if**, **when**, **before**, **after**, **as soon as** and **until**, and in the other part of the sentence we use **will** or **be going to**:

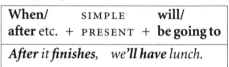

When/ after etc. +	SIMPLE PRESENT +	will/ be going to
After it **finishes**,	*we'll have*	*lunch.*

5 We use the Present Continuous to talk about a future arrangement that we have made with someone else:

A: *Can you come and see us this evening?*
B: *I can't. I'm playing squash with Sam.*

Peter can't come to the cinema with us tonight because he's meeting Jane for dinner.

···

Practice

A   Look at this table and then use *will* and these verbs: *beat, draw with, lose to.*

> *Bob Foster's forecast for next Saturday's big football matches:*
> Arsenal 1, Liverpool 1   Leeds 2, Everton 1   Chelsea 1, Luton 2
> Ipswich 3, Millwall 3   Brighton 2, Oxford 1   Portsmouth 0, Preston 2

Bob Foster thinks that:

0   Arsenal <u>will draw with</u> Liverpool.

1   Leeds _____ Everton.

2   Chelsea _____ Luton.

3   Ipswich _____ Millwall.

4   Brighton _____ Oxford.

5   Portsmouth _____ Preston.

B   In each situation, think about when the person decides to do something. Then complete the sentences using *will* or *be going to* and one of the phrases from the box.

| take it to the car wash | ~~get you an aspirin~~ | see her |
| go to the hairdresser's | have a shower | ~~make some tea~~ |

0   Mary: Philip, I'm very thirsty.

Philip: I am too. I <u>'m going to make some tea</u> . I've already put the kettle on to boil.

0   Sally: What's the matter, Paul?

      Paul: I've got a headache.

      Sally: Oh, I<u>'ll get you an aspirin</u>   .

1   Jack: Is your toothache better?

      Jill: No, but I've phoned the dentist. I _____ at 10.30.

2   Jane: Do you think my hair is all right?

      Sam: No, I'm sorry, I don't. I think it needs a cut.

      Jane: O.K. I _____ this afternoon.

3   Ann: Where's Tom?

      Mike: He's just gone into the bathroom. He _____ .

4   John: Where have you been with the car? It's very dirty.

      Rose: Is it? Okay, I _____ .

C   **Use the words in brackets to write sentences using *will* and the Present Simple.**

0   (Tom/help /us/when/he/come/home)

    <u>Tom will help us when he comes home.</u>

1   (I/buy/the tickets/before/I/go/to work)

    _____

2   (As soon as/Henry/arrive/, we/have/something to eat)

    _____

3   (The play/start/after/the music/stop)

    _____

4   (He/not/stop/until /he/finish/the job)

    _____

5   (When John/get/here, we/go/to the beach)

    _____

D   **Look at Ann's diary for the evenings of next week.**

Monday	8 p.m. play squash with Mary
Tuesday	write some letters
Wednesday	7 p.m. have supper with Jill and Kate
Thursday	tidy my room
Friday	wash my hair
Saturday	6 p.m. meet Tim at the airport

If Ann has an arrangement with someone else, use the Present Continuous, but if she does not, use *be going to*.

0   Ann can't see Fred on Monday because she <u>is playing squash with Mary.</u>

0   She doesn't want to go out on Tuesday because she <u>'s going to write some letters.</u>

1   She won't be at home on Wednesday because she _____

2   On Thursday Ann _____

3   She can't go out on Friday because she _____

4   Ann wants Saturday to come quickly because at 6 p.m. she _____

14 Second conditional (**If he was…**); **I wish I was**

1 Look at this sentence:

*If Charlie Chaplin **was** alive today, he **would be** over 100 years old.*

Of course, Chaplin isn't alive today. The sentence imagines something that is not true. The verb after **if** is Past Simple, but it refers to the present. This structure is called the Second Conditional:

If + PAST SIMPLE + **would** (or **'d**)
*If he **worked** harder, he **would do** better.*

Another example is someone who doesn't have enough money to buy a new car and says:

*I'**d buy** a new car if I **had** enough money.*
Note that we do not use a comma (,) before **if**.

2 We can use the same type of sentence to talk about the future:

If + PAST SIMPLE + **would** (or **'d**)
*If I **won** a lot of money, I'**d buy** a big house.*

This sentence describes an unlikely future situation: it is unlikely that I will win a lot of money.

3 We can use **wish** to say that we want something to be different from how it is now. Note that the verb after **wish** is past (e.g. **could, was, had**):

I wish you could talk

*I **wish** (that) Chaplin **was** still alive.*
*Mary **wishes** she **had** enough money for a new dress.*
*I **wish** I **was** very rich.*

4 After **if** and after **wish**, we sometimes use **I/he/she/it** with **were**:

*If he **were** (or was) alive today,…*
*I **wish** Charlie Chaplin **were** (or was) still alive.*

Notice also the expression **if I were you**, when you give someone advice:

*If I **were you**, I'**d go** to the police.*
(Not *If I was you,…*)

• •

Practice

A **Complete these sentences.**

0 If Sally lived in Brighton, <u>she would be</u> (she/be) near her parents.

0 Fred would read more if <u>he didn't work</u> (he/not/work) so hard.

1 If Elizabeth didn't have to work in the evenings, _____ (she/go) to concerts.

2 Susan wouldn't go to work by car if _____ (she/live) near a train station.

3 Alan wouldn't be fat if _____ (he/not/eat) so much.

4 If Peter didn't live in a flat, _____ (he/have) a dog.

5 Pam would definitely learn French if _____ (she/get) a job in France.

6 If Mark wanted to be healthy, _____ (he/not/smoke).

B **In the next few years:**

> It is unlikely that astronauts will visit Mars.
> ~~It is unlikely that governments will stop buying guns.~~
> It is unlikely that doctors will find a cure for cancer.
> It is unlikely that they will discover oil in Ireland.
> It is unlikely that young people will stop buying pop records.

Now use the predictions in the box to complete these sentences.

0 If _governments stopped buying guns_ , the world would be safer.

1 If _____ , the Irish would be very happy.

2 If _____ , this terrible disease would disappear.

3 If _____ , the popular music industry would disappear.

4 If _____ , we would learn a lot about the planet.

C **A manager tells people why they can't have a job. Write their thoughts with _I wish_.**

0 You don't have a driving licence, so you can't have the job.
   I wish _I had a driving licence._

0 You can't have the job because you can't type.
   I wish _I could type._

1 You can't have the job because you don't have good eyesight.
   I wish _____

2 You can't speak German, so you can't have the job.
   I wish _____

3 You don't have a degree, so you can't have the job.
   I wish _____

4 You can't have the job because you are not 18.
   I wish _____

D **Imagine how life nowadays could be better. Complete the sentences using the words in brackets, and any other words you need.**

0 People don't do enough exercise, so there is a lot of heart disease.
   (more, less) If people _did more exercise_ , there _would be less heart disease_ .

1 There are too many cars. The city is very polluted.
   (fewer) I wish there _____ , then the city wouldn't be very polluted.

2 People drive too fast, so there are a lot of accidents.
   (more slowly) I wish people _____ , then there would be fewer accidents.

3 People watch too much TV, so they don't have much time for reading.
   (more) If people watched less TV, they _____ .

4 Children have bad teeth because they eat too many sweets.
   (fewer) Children would have better teeth if they _____ .

5 Not enough people travel by bus, so the roads are crowded.
   (more) I wish _____ , then the roads would be less crowded.

6 People haven't got enough time to cook, so they eat a lot of 'fast food'.
   (more, less) If people _____ , they _____

15 Third conditional (**If he had been…**); **I wish I had been…**

1 Look at this sentence:

*If Charlie Chaplin **had died** in 1989, he **would have been** 100 years old.*

Chaplin did not in fact die in 1989. He died before he was 100 years old. The sentence imagines something that did not happen in the past. This structure is called the Third Conditional:

If + PAST PERFECT + { **would have** (or **'d have**)
*If he **had tried** harder,*   *he **would have** won.*

Here is another example:

*If Jane **had come** on her usual train, I **would have seen** her.* (She **didn't come** on her usual train, so I **didn't see** her.)

Notice how we can also use the negative forms **wouldn't have** and **hadn't**:

*John F. Kennedy **wouldn't have died** in 1963 if he **hadn't gone** to Dallas.* (Kennedy **died** in 1963 because he **went** to Dallas, but this sentence imagines the opposite).

*I would have phoned you if I **hadn't lost** your phone number.* (I didn't phone you because I lost your phone number.)

*I **wouldn't have gone** to the museum if I had known it was shut.* (I went to the museum because I didn't know it was shut.)

2 We can use **wish** + **had done** to talk about the past when we are sorry that something didn't happen, and we imagine that it did:

*He **wishes** he **had studied** hard at school.* (He **didn't study** hard, and now he's sorry about it.)

*I woke up very late this morning. I **wish** I **had gone** to bed earlier last night.*

We can use a negative form (**wish…hadn't done**) to say that we are sorry that something did happen:

*Many people **wish** that John F. Kennedy **hadn't gone** to Dallas.* (Many people are sorry that John F. Kennedy **went** to Dallas.)

....

Practice

A Read this story about Ellen.

> In May 1992 Ellen lost her job in London. She didn't have much money in the bank, so she was very worried. She looked in the newspapers and she saw an advertisement for a job as a translator from German into English. She didn't speak German very well, so she didn't apply for it. In June, she heard about some teaching jobs abroad because a friend phoned to tell her about them. She phoned the company, and they asked her to go for an interview with the director. Ellen thought the interview went badly, but in fact the director was happy with the interview and offered Ellen a job in Spain. However, Ellen couldn't start at once because she didn't know any Spanish. She took a course to learn the language. She was good at languages and she made rapid progress. So, by September she had a new job, and she still had a little money left in the bank.

Now write sentences using the words in brackets.

0 (If Ellen/have/a lot of money in the bank, she/not/be/ so worried)

  If Ellen had had a lot of money in the bank, she wouldn't have been so worried.

0 (If she/not/look/in the newspapers, she/not/see/the advertisement)

  If she hadn't looked in the newspapers, she wouldn't have seen the advertisement.

1 (If she/speak/German very well, she/apply/for the job)

   _____

2 (If her friend/not/phone, she /not/hear/about the teaching jobs)

   _____

3 (If she/not/contact/the company, they/not/ask/her to go for an interview)

   _____

4 (If the interview/go/badly, the director/not/offer/Ellen a job)

   _____

5 (If Ellen/know/some Spanish, she/start/at once)

   _____

6 (If she/not/be/good at languages, she/not/make/rapid progress)

   _____

B **Use the information in brackets ( ) to complete these sentences.**

   0 (Sam didn't get the job as a translator because he failed the exam.)

   Sam _would have got_ the job as a translator if he _had_ not _failed_ the exam.

   1 (Alan lost our phone number, so he didn't phone us.)

   If Alan _____ not _____ our phone number, he _____ us.

   2 (Sally broke her leg, so she didn't go on holiday.)

   If Sally _____ not _____ her leg, she _____ on holiday.

   3 (We didn't make a cake because we forgot to buy any eggs.)

   We _____ a cake if we _____ not _____ to buy some eggs.

C **Write sentences about these people who are sorry about things they did in the past. Use wish or wishes.**

   0 Ian wasted his time at school; now he's sorry.

   Ian wishes he hadn't wasted his time at school.

   1 I didn't tell the truth; now I'm sorry.

   I wish _____

   2 John borrowed some money from his mother; now he's sorry.

   John _____

   3 Mary didn't get up early; now she's sorry.

   Mary _____

   4 Peter didn't go to the party; now he's sorry.

   Peter _____

   5 I didn't send Jill a birthday card; now I'm sorry.

   I _____

   6 Fiona didn't help her sister; now she's sorry.

   _____

   7 He shouted at the children; now he's sorry.

   _____

16 Zero, first and second conditionals

1 ZERO CONDITIONAL

If + PRESENT SIMPLE + { PRESENT SIMPLE
If you **eat** too much, you **get** fat.

We use **if** + Present Simple + Present Simple to talk about something that is true at any time:
> If something **is** lighter than water, it **floats**.
> I **don't cycle** to work if it**'s** very cold.

2 FIRST CONDITIONAL

If + PRESENT SIMPLE + will (or 'll)
If I **see** Ann, I**'ll invite** her.

We use **if** + Present Simple + **will** to talk about things that are possible in the future:
> We **will go** to the beach this Saturday if the weather **is** hot enough. (= It's possible it will be hot.)

Note that in this sentence there is a possibility and a result:

future possibility + result
If it's hot, we will go to the beach.

If the result is only possible, not certain, we use **might** (not ~~will~~):
> If it's hot, we **might** go to the beach.
> (= It is possible that we will go to the beach if it's hot.)

We can use **unless** to mean 'if...not':
> We will go to the mountains on Saturday **unless** it rains. (=...if it doesn't rain.)
> **Unless** you pay for the broken window, I'll phone the police. (= If you don't pay,...)

3 SECOND CONDITIONAL

If + PAST SIMPLE + would (or 'd)
If he **worked** less, he**'d enjoy** life more.

We use **if** + Past Simple + **would** to talk about the present, and to imagine something different from the real situation now:
> If Shakespeare was alive today, what **would** he **write** about? (Shakespeare isn't alive today.)
> If animals **could** speak, we **would be** able to discover what they think. (We aren't able to discover what animals think, because they can't speak.)
> If he **didn't live** so close to his office, he **wouldn't be** able to stay in bed so late in the morning.

We can also use the second conditional to talk about an unlikely situation in the future:
> If all the ice in the world **melted**, many coastal towns **would disappear**.

....

Practice

A Write what happens when you heat these things, as in the example.

0 The boiling point of water is 100 degrees centigrade.
> _So if you heat water to 100 degrees, it boils._

1 The melting point of gold is 1063 degrees centigrade.
So _____

2 The boiling point of alcohol is 78 degrees.
So _____

3 The melting point of silver is 960 degrees.
So _____

B Complete each sentence using the verb in brackets in the Present Simple or with *will*, as in the examples.

0 If she ___wins___ (win) a prize, Mary ___will be___ (be) very happy.

1 If John _____ (come) this weekend, we _____ (go) to the theatre.

2 If Ann _____ (write) to me, I _____ (tell) you what she says.

3   My father _____ (forgive) Susan if she _____ (pay) for the broken window.

4   Jack _____ (feel) a lot better if he _____ (stop) smoking.

5   If Bob _____ (need) some money, we _____ (lend) him some.

6   If Mark _____ (listen) to the instructions, he _____ (know) what to do.

C   Put *will* or *might* in the gaps.

0   If Mary comes, I ____will____ definitely tell her what happened.

0   I ____might____ change my car if I get a better job, but I'm not sure.

1   Alan hasn't decided but he thinks that if his health doesn't improve, he _____ move to another town.

2   Rose has decided what to do; if Tom doesn't want to go to the museum, she _____ go there alone.

3   We've decided; we _____ lend them our car if they pay for the petrol.

4   I'm not sure. If I win some money, I _____ take a holiday, or I _____ put the money in the bank.

D   Rewrite the <u>underlined</u> words using the words in brackets.

0   They won't let her in to the concert <u>unless she has a ticket</u>.
    (if) They won't let her in _if she doesn't have a ticket._

0   We won't go and see that film <u>if you don't want to</u>.
    (unless) We won't go and see that film _unless you want to._

1   The doctor will not see you <u>if you do not telephone first</u>.
    (unless) The doctor will not see you _____

2   You can't go and stay at the Johnsons' <u>unless they invite you</u>.
    (if) You can't go and stay at the Johnsons' _____

3   You can't be a sailor <u>unless you can swim</u>.
    (if) You can't be a sailor _____

4   Our team will be in trouble <u>if we don't win on Saturday</u>.
    (unless) Our team will be in trouble _____

E   Use each statement in brackets ( ) to complete each sentence. Use *wouldn't be able to*.

0   (Cats have very good eyes; that's why they can see in the dark.)
    If cats didn't have very good eyes, they _wouldn't be able to see in the dark._

1   (Bats have very good ears; that's how they move about so easily in the dark.)
    If bats didn't have very good ears, they _____

2   (Dogs are able to recognize people because they have a good sense of smell.)
    Dogs _____ if they didn't have a good sense of smell.

3   (We can train dogs; that's why they are able to help blind people.)
    If we couldn't train dogs, they _____

4   (Elephants remember everything because they have good memories.)
    Elephants _____ if they didn't have good memories.

5   (Horses can pull heavy loads because they are very strong.)
    _____ if they weren't very strong.

17 Uses of **get**, **do** and **make**

1 **Get** has many meanings; here are some of the most common ones:
- ▶ **have got** = 'have':
  Have you **got** any brothers or sisters?
- ▶ **get** (+ noun) = 'receive':
  Did you **get** any letters today?
  She **got** a dictionary for her birthday.
- ▶ **get** (+ noun) = 'obtain', 'buy':
  Could you **get** a pen from my desk?
  I'll **get** some cheese when I go to the shops.
- ▶ **get to** (+ noun) = 'arrive at/in':
  What time did you **get to** the office?
- ▶ **get** (+ adjective) = 'become':
  Everything is **getting** more expensive.
  It was very hot and we **got** very thirsty.

Study these examples of **get** + adjective:

get dressed	get divorced
get undressed	get confused
get washed	get lost
get engaged	get drunk
get married	get stuck

2 Look at these examples of **do** and **make**:
A: *What's Jim **doing**?*
B: *He's **making** a cake.* (Not ~~doing~~)
A: *What sort of cake is he **making**?*
B: *A chocolate cake.*
A: *What's Helen **making**?*
B: *She isn't **making** anything.*
A: *What's Helen **doing** then?*
B: *She's reading.*
We usually use **do** for action in general, but **make** means 'produce': e.g. *make bread*.

3 Here are some common uses of **do**:

do your best	do some work
do an exercise	do some homework
do her hair	do a job
do the washing up	do someone a favour
do the cleaning	do the shopping

Here are some common uses of **make**:

make a complaint	make a decision
make a difference	make an effort
make friends	make a journey
make a meal	make a mistake

Practice

A Complete the sentences using another verb instead of *get*.

0 Mary got a prize for her drawing.
Mary <u>received</u> a prize for her drawing.

1 What time does this train get to London?
What time does this train ＿＿＿＿＿＿ in London?

2 The noise got louder and louder.
The noise ＿＿＿＿＿＿ louder and louder.

3 Will you get some fruit when you go to the shops?
Will you ＿＿＿＿＿＿ some fruit when you go to the shops?

4 Peter got a phone call from Japan this morning.
Peter ＿＿＿＿＿＿ a phone call from Japan this morning.

5 We usually get our meat from the supermarket.
We usually ＿＿＿＿＿＿ our meat from the supermarket.

6 They will get a cheque for the work they have done.
They will ＿＿＿＿＿＿ a cheque for the work they have done.

7 In the middle of the day the desert sand gets very hot.
In the middle of the day the desert sand ＿＿＿＿＿＿ very hot.

8 We got to the station after our train had left.
We ＿＿＿＿＿＿ at the station after our train had left.

B **Put in a suitable phrase with _get_ and one of the words in the box.**

| confused | divorced | ~~dressed~~ | drunk | engaged |
| lost | married | stuck | undressed | washed |

0   When you've finished swimming, _get dressed_____ quickly so you don't get cold.

1   Jane and Bill were engaged for 3 years. They _____ in 1987 and they
_____ in 1990. But they were only married for 2 years because they
_____ in 1992.

2   The doctor would like to examine you all over. Can you _____, please?

3   They took their car onto the beach and it _____ in the sand.

4   Don't go through the woods; follow the road and you won't _____.

5   I'm very dirty; I must go and _____.

6   Football hooligans often go to pubs and _____ before the match starts.

7   When people explain things too quickly to me, I often _____.

C **Maria is fifteen and she is talking about her family. Put in the right form of _do_ or _make_.**

In our house there is always plenty of work ⁰ _to do_____ . Luckily, everybody ¹ _____
something. For example, my big brother ² _____ the shopping; my twin sister
³ _____ the toast for breakfast, and on Sundays she ⁴ _____ pancakes. My parents
usually ⁵ _____ the supper, and I always ⁶ _____ the washing-up. At the
weekends, we all ⁷ _____ the cleaning - except for my baby sister because she's too small to
⁸ _____ anything.

D **Put the right form of _do_ or _make_ and one of the words in the box into the conversation.**

| best | ~~favour~~ | difference | effort | decision |
| friends | job | ~~shopping~~ | work | mistake |

Rose: Would you ⁰ _do me a favour_ and ⁰ _do_ some _shopping_ for me today?

Alan: Yes, okay.

Rose: Are you all right, Alan? Is something wrong?

Alan: I have to ¹ _____ a difficult _____ about my future. I think I'm going to leave my
job.

Rose: What's the matter at work? Are the people there not nice? Haven't you
² _____ any _____ there?

Alan: Oh, yes. I like the people who work there.

Rose: What is it then?

Alan: Well, I think I ³ _____ a _____ when I chose an office job because I have to
⁴ _____ all the boring _____, and I don't like it.

Rose: When you start, it doesn't ⁵ _____ much _____ what kind of company it is. New
people often have to ⁶ _____ a boring _____ at first. You just have to
⁷ _____ your _____ and when they see that you are ⁸ _____ an _____, then
perhaps they'll offer you something better.

18 Phrasal verbs (**look for, put on, get up**)

1 We can use many verbs with other words to make a phrasal verb, e.g. **look for**, **put on**, **get up**.

2 One verb can go with several other words to make different phrasal verbs: **go with**, **go off**, **go on**. The meaning of the phrasal verb is not always clear from the two parts. For example, **go on** means 'continue'. You should check the meaning of phrasal verbs in a dictionary.

3 Grammatically, there are three different groups of phrasal verbs.

> ▶ Group 1:
> *The police are **looking for** the criminal.*
> *The police are **looking for** him.*
> (Not *They are looking him for.*)
> **Look for** has an object (**the criminal**, **him**). Note that the object goes after the phrasal verb. Some common verbs in this group are:

agree with	ask for	feel like
look after	look at	look for
get at	join in	call for

> ▶ Group 2:
> *She **put on** a hat.*
> *She **put** a hat **on**.*
> *She **put** it **on**.* (Not *She put on it.*)
> **Put on** has an object (**a hat**, **it**). If the object is a pronoun (**me, you, her, him, it, us, them, one, some, any**), then it goes in the middle of the phrasal verb; if the object is a noun, it can go either after the verb or in the middle. Some common verbs in this group are:

bring back	draw out	put on
fill in	take off	put away
hand in	rub out	look up
let out	turn down/off	

> ▶ Group 3:
> *I usually **get up** at 7 o'clock.*
> **Get up** is a phrasal verb that does not have an object. Some common verbs in this group are:

come round	get away	get back
go on	get off	get up
hold on (=wait)	go off	go out

Practice

A Use the phrasal verbs in the box in the correct form to complete the conversation between Frank and his daughter Anna.

go out (= leave a building/room)	come round (= visit)	join in (= take part in)
~~turn down~~ (= lower, make quieter)	get back (= return)	call for (= collect)
get off (= leave a bus/train/plane)	look after (= care for)	put on (= wear)

Frank: Anna, ⁰ <u>turn down</u> the music a bit. I want to tell you something.

Anna: What is it?

Frank: Tom has just phoned to say that he is ¹_____ here with his children, Jane and Michael. He wants us to ²_____ them while he goes to the shops in the centre of town.

Anna: We don't have to stay at home, do we? I'm going to the sports club with Sally. She's ³_____ me at 11 o'clock.

Frank: No, you can ⁴_____ if you like. But it's cold; are you going to go on your bike?

Anna: Yes, but I'll ⁵_____ some warm clothes.

Frank: Okay, Jane and Michael can go there on the bus. I'll tell them where to

⁶_____ . And when you're at the club, can you let Jane and Michael

⁷_____ your games.

Anna: Don't worry. We always have a good time together.

Frank: Good, but remember to ⁸_____ by 1 o'clock, because that's when
we're having lunch.

B **In each sentence, replace the <u>underlined</u> words with a phrasal verb from the box that means the same. Use a dictionary to help you.**

brought back	~~get away~~	went off	fill in	get at
hold on	look up	put away	rubbed out	

0 How did the prisoners <u>escape</u>?   _get away_____

1 If you want a passport, you must <u>complete</u> this form.   _____

2 <u>Wait</u>! I'm coming.   _____

3 I can't <u>reach</u> the books at the back of the cupboard.   _____

4 The bomb <u>exploded</u> just before midnight   _____

5 The teacher <u>erased</u> the words that were wrong.   _____

6 You can <u>consult</u> the meaning of the words in a dictionary.   _____

7 Has Philip <u>returned</u> the books that he borrowed?   _____

8 At the end of the day the children <u>stored</u> their toys.   _____

C **Complete these short dialogues with a sentence that has a phrasal verb, in the correct tense, and the word in brackets( ).**

0 Anna: Have you taken your shoes off?

  Carol: (them) Yes, I've _taken them off._____

0 Jane: We must ask for some more paper.

  Dennis: (some) I'll _ask for some_____ tomorrow.

1 Tom: Have you looked for your keys?

  Ann: (them) Yes, I've _____ everywhere.

2 Jeff: Can you turn the bedroom lights off, please?

  Harry: (them) Yes, I'll _____ in a minute.

3 Olive: Have the students handed in their homework?

  Pam: (it) Yes, they've all _____.

4 Ken: Do you agree with Tom?

  Ben: (him) No, I never _____.

5 Susan: When did you draw the money out of your bank account?

  Noel: (it) I _____ of my account yesterday.

6 Karen: When did you let the cat out into the garden?

  Sally: (it) I _____ into the garden, before I went to bed.

19 Can, could, be able to, may, will, shall

1 We use **can**, **could**, **be able to** and **may** with an infinitive (e.g. **be**, **go**, **swim**):

	INFINITIVE
She can	*swim.*

2 ABILITY

She { *can/could* / *will be able to* }	*swim.*

Joy can swim 1,000 metres now.
Last year she couldn't swim at all.
She'll be able to swim the English Channel soon.

When we talk about a person's ability to do something, we normally use **can** (negative **cannot** or **can't**) for present time, **could** for past time, and **will be able to** for future time.

In past time, we do not normally use could for something that happened on a particular occasion. We use **was able to** or **managed**:

> *The boat was in difficulties, but in the end it managed to reach the port. (or…it was able to reach…; not …it could reach…)*

3 PERMISSION

Can I / *Could I* / *May I*	*leave this here?*

We use **Can I** etc. to ask for permission. Note that **Could I** and **May I** are more formal and polite than **Can I**.

We use **can** or **may** to give permission:
> *You can leave your bag here. (or…may leave…)*

If we talk about what is allowed in general (i.e., not by a particular person), we use **can**:
> *People can drive on the roads when they are 17.*

But official notices often use **may**:
> *BAGS MAY BE LEFT HERE.*

4 REQUESTS

Can you / *Could you* / *Would you*	*help me?*

We use **Can you**, **Could you**, and **Would you**, (but not **May you**) when we ask someone to do something. **Could** and **would** are more formal and polite than **can**.

5 OFFERS

I'll do it.
Shall I do it?

I'll post that letter for you.
Shall I open the door?
We use **shall I** and **I'll** to offer to do something. Note that **shall I** is a question:
> A: *Shall I open the door?*
> B: *Yes, please ./No, thank you.*

....

Practice

A Look at this table and complete the sentences using *can*, *could*, or *will be able to*.

	last year	now	hopes for the future
Joy	swim 100 metres	swim 1000 metres	swim for her club team
Mark	type 15 words per minute	type 30 words per minute	work as a secretary
Bill	lift 25 kilos	lift 100 kilos	join a weightlifting team
Anne	speak only a little French	speak French quite well	work as an interpreter
Carol	only cook omelettes	cook quite well	work as a chef
Tom	only play the piano	play the piano and the violin	be a professional musician
Susan	ride a bike	drive a car	drive a racing car

0   Last year Joy ___could swim 100 metres___. Now, ___she can swim 1000 metres___.

0   At the moment Anne ___can speak French___ quite well, and if she studies hard,

perhaps ___she'll be able to work___ as an interpreter.

1   Last year Mark _____. Now, _____.

2   At the moment Bill _____, and if he trains hard, perhaps

_____.

3   Last year Anne _____. Now, _____.

4   At the moment Carol _____, and if she works hard, perhaps

      _____.

5   Last year Tom _____. Now, _____,

      and if he studies hard, perhaps _____.

6   Last year Susan _____. Now, _____,

      and she hopes that one day _____.

B **Choose the right word from the words in brackets, and put it in the gap.**

0   __May__ (May/Will/Would) I take one of these forms, please?

1   In the street:

    Excuse me, officer, __could__ (could/may/shall) you tell me how to

    get to the station?

2   In an office:

    A: __Could/would__ (Shall/Could/Would) I speak to Mrs Timms, please?

    B: I'm afraid she's in a meeting.

    A: I see. __Shall__ (Will/Would/Shall) I come back later?

    B: Yes, come back in about an hour.

3   At a railway station:

    A: Do you think we __can__ (may/can/would) eat our sandwiches

      here?

    B: __Can't__ (Couldn't/Can't/Wouldn't) you read? Look at the notice;

      it says: 'FOOD __could__ (WOULD/MAY/COULD) NOT BE

      EATEN IN THIS WAITING ROOM.'

4   A: Somebody must tell Jenny about next week's meeting.

    B: __Shall__ (Will/Would/Shall) I phone her?

    A: No, you __can't__ (may not/can't/will not) phone her because she

      hasn't got a phone.

    B: Oh, I see. Tell me her address again, and I __'ll__ (may/'ll) take

      a message to her.

    A: Are you sure you __'ll be able to__ (could/may/'ll be able to) find her

      house?

    B: Well, I __could__ (could/would/managed to) find it the last time

      that I went there, without any problem.

5   A: __May/Could__ (May/Could/Shall) someone help me?

    B: What __would__ (would/can) I do to help you?

    A: We need to move the chairs and to clean this room. Can you help?

    B: I'm afraid I __can't__ (may not/can't/would not) move the chairs

      because of my bad back. But __I'll__ (I'll/will I/shall I) do the

      cleaning for you if you like.

20 Probability: **must, can't, may, might, could**

1 We use **must**, **can't**, **may** and **could** with an infinitive (e.g. **be**, **go**, **come**, **earn**):

	INFINITIVE	
*They **must***	***earn***	*a lot.*

2 CERTAINTY | *She **must be** rich.* |

Look at this example with **must**:

*Jane got top marks in her exams. She **must be** very clever.* (= From what we know, we can be certain that Jane is very clever.)

We use **must** to say we are certain:

*The Greens have two houses and two cars. They **must earn** a lot of money.* (= We can be sure that the Greens earn a lot of money.)

A: *There's someone outside in an orange car.*
B: *It **must be** Susan. She's the only person I know with an orange car.*

3 IMPOSSIBILITY | *She **can't be** poor.* |

Look at this example with **can't**:

*Mark studied hard for his exams, but he got poor marks; he **can't be** very clever.* (= From what we know, we can guess that Mark is **not** very clever.)

We use **can't** to talk about impossibility:

*The Browns both have part-time jobs; they **can't earn** much money.* (= We can guess that the Browns do **not** earn a lot of money.)

A: *There's someone at the door. I think it's Bill.*
B: *It **can't be** Bill. He's in Australia.*

3 POSSIBILITY

She	*may* *might* *could*	*be in the garden.*

Look at this example with **may**:

A: *Eve's not in her room. Where is she?*
B: *She **may be** in the garden.*
(= From what we know, **perhaps** she **is** in the garden.)

We use **may**, **might** and **could** for something that is possible but not certain, now or in the future:

*My sister **might come** tomorrow.*
(= From what we know, perhaps she **will** come.)

Now look at this example with **may not**:

A: *I've phoned Jill, but there's no answer.*
B: *She **may not be** at home.* (or *She **might not be**…*)
(= Perhaps she is not at home.)

Could not is not possible here.

....

Practice

A Complete the sentences using *must* or *can't* and one of the verbs from the box.

~~be~~ belong ~~speak~~ come spend have like live want remember

0 Anna lived in America for three years, so she <u>must speak</u> English.

0 Tom's brother doesn't know anything about medicine, so he <u>can't be</u> a doctor.

1 Jane has an incredible number of compact discs. She _____ music a lot.

2 Peter doesn't speak German, so he _____ from Germany.

3 This jacket _____ to Janet because it's not her size.

4 That man _____ around here because he doesn't know any of the street names.

5 Jack _____ a lot of clothes. He wears something different every day.

6 Sam's grandmother is over eighty years old, so she _____ the Second World War.

7 You've got ten cats already. You _____ to get another one.

8 Susan buys a new dress every day. She _____ a lot of money on clothes.

B Someone has robbed a bank. The police are sure that the criminal is one of these men. Look at the pictures and complete the sentences using *can't be*, *could be*, or *must be*.

Drake   Hall   Brown   Rogers   Smith

0 A witness says that the robber had short hair. If that's true, then it __can't be__ Drake or Rogers, but it __could be__ Hall.

0 A witness says that the robber had glasses. If that's true, then it __can't be__ Brown or Drake. It __must be__ either Hall or Rogers or Smith.

1 A witness says that the robber had black hair. If that's true, then it _____ Hall, but it _____ Brown.

2 A witness says that the robber had a moustache. If that's true, then it _____ Rogers but it _____ Drake or Brown.

3 A witness says that the robber didn't have a beard. If that's true, then it _____ Drake or Brown but it _____ Hall or Smith.

4 A witness says that the robber had a moustache, but no beard. If that's true, then it _____ Drake or Rogers. It _____ Hall.

5 A witness says that the robber had black hair and wore glasses. If that's true, then it _____ Rogers. It _____ Hall.

6 And if what everyone says is true, then it _____.

C Complete the dialogues with *must*, *can't* or *might* and one of the phrases in the box.

cost a lot of money	~~be a soldier~~	work long hours
go to Portugal	come this weekend	take much interest
also be at the shops	be at the gym	

0 Ruth: I think Ann's brother is in the army.
  James: He __can't be a soldier__; he's only 15.

1 Bob: What are you going to do next summer?
  Susan: I don't know. We _____, but it's not certain yet.

2 Fred: Mike's new flat is all electric—kitchen, heating, everything.
  Peter: That _____ in electricity bills.

3 Sam: Is Mary coming to see us this week?
  Sally: It depends on her work. She _____ if she finishes the project that she's doing.

4 Carol: Have Brian and Kim got any children?
  Tom: Yes, they have two children, but they _____ in them, because they never talk about them.

5 Andrew: Do you see your new neighbours very much?
  Sarah: No, they _____, because they are hardly ever at home.

6 Paul: Fred's gone out, hasn't he? Where has he gone?
  Ann: I don't know. He _____ or he _____.

21 Obligation: must, have to, mustn't, don't have to

Dec 8

1 We use **must** when we think it is important to do an action:

*You **must go**.* (= It is important that you go.)
We make negatives, questions and short answers like this:
*You **mustn't go**.*
***Must** you **go**? ~ Yes, I **must**.*

2 We use **have to** to talk about an action that is necessary because of rules or laws, or because someone obliges us to do it:

*Doctors sometimes **have to work** on Sunday.* (It is in the rules of their work.)
We make negatives, questions and short answers with a form of **do**:
*Teachers **don't have to work** on Sunday.*
***Do** you **have to work** today? ~ No, I **don't**.*

3 POSITIVE
In positive sentences we can often use **must** and **have to** with little difference in meaning, because many things are important both because we think so and because there are rules:

*In Britain you **must drive** on the left.* (or
*…you **have to drive** …*)
(= It is obligatory to drive on the left.)

4 NEGATIVE
Note the difference in meaning between **mustn't** and **don't have to**.
In negative sentences we often use **mustn't** to say that something is against the rules, or against the law:

*You **mustn't smoke** on buses.*
(Smoking is against the rules.)
*In football you **mustn't touch** the ball with your hands.* (Touching the ball is against the rules.)

We use **don't have to** to say that people are not obliged to do something:

*In Britain, people **don't have to carry** a passport with them.* (= People are not obliged to carry one.)
*Nowadays pupils **do not have to learn** Latin at school.* (= They are not obliged to learn it.)

5 QUESTIONS
In questions we usually use **do/does…have to** (not ~~must~~) to ask if something is obligatory or important:

***Does** Michael **have to get** up early tomorrow?*
***Do** we **have to wait** here?*

....

Practice

A Make these sentences negative, as in the examples.

0   They must come today.   They mustn't come today.
0   Tim has to stay at home.   Tim doesn't have to stay at home.
1   They have to go now.   _____
2   Mark must speak to my cousin.   _____
3   You have to drive slowly here.   _____
4   Alice has to get up early.   _____
5   The children must play in the park. _____
6   Mike has to phone his brother.   _____

B From the statements in brackets, make a question using *Do /Does…have to* and a short answer, as in the examples.

0 (They don't have to work hard.) Do they have to work hard ____ ? ~ No, they don't.
0 (They must stay at home.) Do they have to stay at home ____ ? ~ Yes, they do.
1 (Jim has to go to the doctor's.) _____ ? ~ Yes, _____
2 (We must show our passports.) _____ ? ~ Yes, _____

3 (Linda doesn't have to pay.) _____? ~ No, _____

4 (They must do all this work today.) _____? ~ Yes, _____

C Put *must* or *mustn't* and one of the verbs in the box in the sentences.

| be | ~~drive~~ | obey | park | play | work |

0 Car drivers _must drive_____ slowly in towns.

1 You _____ your car in a 'No Parking' area.

2 Everybody _____ the traffic police.

3 You _____ football in the street.

4 Drivers _____ careful when it's foggy.

5 Lorry drivers _____ when they are tired.

D The Stanton Squash Club has decided that it is important for all club members to do these things:

| wear sports shoes and clean clothes | have a shower |
| pay before you play | finish on time |

But these things are not allowed:

| disturb other players | eat or drink outside the bar |
| take club balls home | |

Put *have to*, *don't have to*, or *mustn't* in the gaps.

0 You _don't have to_____ wear white clothes, but you _have to_____ wear sports shoes.

0 You _mustn't_____ disturb other players, but you _don't have to_____ be silent.

1 You _____ finish on time, but you _____ start on time.

2 You _____ play with club balls, but if you do, you _____ take them home.

3 You _____ eat or drink outside the bar, but you _____ buy your food in the bar if you don't want to.

4 You _____ have a shower, and you _____ wear clean clothes.

E Put the words in the box in the gaps. Don't add any other words.

| Does she | have to | has | she has |
| must | mustn't | ~~have~~ | does she |

Mark: We 0 _have_____ to get up early tomorrow.

Bob: Why?

Mark: Have you forgotten? Angela 1_____ to move to a new flat tomorrow, and I promised we would help her.

Bob: 2_____ have to move out by a particular time?

Mark: No, there's no rush. She doesn't 3_____ leave her old flat before the afternoon, but there are lots of things that 4_____ to pack, so we 5_____ get there fairly early.

Bob: Why 6_____ have to move, by the way?

Mark: She said that I 7_____ tell you because she wants to tell you herself, when she sees you tomorrow.

22 Necessity: **need, needn't, needn't have**

1 We use the verb **need** to talk about things that we must do. We use **to** + infinitive (e.g. **to do**, **to go**) after **need**:

to + INFINITIVE	
I **need**	**to go**	to the dentist's.

After **he/she/it** we use **needs**:
*Mary /she **needs to buy** some white paint.*

We make negatives, questions, and short answers with a form of **do**:
*You **don't need to go** to the doctor's.*
*Mary **doesn't need to buy** any green paint.*
A: *Do you **need to go** to the dentist's?*
B: *Yes, I **do**./No, I **don't**.*
A: *Does Mary **need to buy** any brushes?*
B: *Yes, she **does**./No, she **doesn't**.*

2 We can also use **need** to talk about things that we must get. Here we use an object after **need**:

	OBJECT
Mary **needs**	some white paint
I **don't need**	a new car.
Does Peter **need**	any help?

3 To talk about what we do not need to do, we can use **needn't**. We use an infinitive (e.g. **go**, **buy**) after **needn't**. **Needn't** has the same meaning as **don't/doesn't need to**:

INFINITIVE	
You **needn't**	**go**	to the shops. We have

enough food.
(Or *You **don't need to go** to the shops.*)
*Mary **needn't buy** any paint.*
(Or *Mary **doesn't need to buy** any paint.*)

We cannot use **needn't** before an object (e.g. **your coat**); we must use **don't need**:
*You **don't need** your coat. It's not cold outside.*
(Not ~~You **needn't** your coat.~~)

4 We can use **needed to** for past time:
*They **needed to clean** everything before they started to paint.*
Notice the meaning of **needn't have done**:
*We **needn't have lit** the fire, because it was a warm evening.*
(= We lit the fire, but it was not necessary to light it.)
*You **needn't have bought** any bread, Jim. There is plenty in the cupboard.*
(= You bought some bread, but it was not necessary.)

....

Practice

A **From the statements in brackets, make a question and a short answer, like those in the examples.**

0 (Tom needs to take some warm clothes.) <u>Does Tom need to take some warm clothes?</u>

~ Yes, <u>he does.</u>

0 (She doesn't need to study hard.) <u>Does she need to study hard?</u> ~ No, <u>she doesn't.</u>

1 (Fred needs a ladder.) _____ ?~ Yes, _____.

2 (We don't need to go to the shops.) _____ ?~ No, _____.

3 (John doesn't need to leave before lunch.) _____ ?~ No, _____.

4 (They need to check the train times.) _____ ?~ Yes, _____.

B **Change each sentence in brackets ( ) into a negative sentence with *needn't*, where possible. If not possible, write a negative sentence with *doesn't/don't need*.**

0 (Jane needs to pay Jim today.) <u>Jane needn't pay Jim today.</u>

0 (The car needs new tyres.) <u>The car doesn't need new tyres.</u>

1 (We need a lot of red paper.) _____

2 (Mark needs to get everything ready today.) _____

3　(Mary needs to leave at six o'clock.) _____

4　(Ann needs a new bag.) _____

C　**When there are exams or competitions at Brightside School, the school provides certain things for all the students, but there are other things that the school does not provide. Look at the table.**

Examinations	The school provides:	The school doesn't provide:
art exams	paint	brushes
maths exams	rubbers	pens and pencils
drawing exams	paper	rulers and pencils
tennis competitions	balls	racquets
football competitions	shirts	shorts and boots

Use the information in the table to write sentences with *need to bring* or *needn't bring*.

0　(art exams/paint) _For art exams, students needn't bring paint._

0　(tennis competitions/racquets) _For tennis competitions, students need to bring racquets._

1　(maths exams/pens and pencils) _____

2　(football competitions/shirts) _____

3　(drawing exams/paper) _____

4　(art exams/brushes) _____

5　(tennis competitions/balls) _____

6　(football competitions/shorts and boots) _____

7　(maths exams/ rubbers) _____

8　(drawing exams/rulers and pencils) _____

D　**Rewrite what each person says using *needn't* + verb, or *needn't have* + verb.**

0　(Jane:　You don't need to go to the passport office, Bob, to get a new passport. It says here that they send it to you in the post.)

　　Jane:　You _needn't go_ to the passport office, Bob, to get a new passport.

0　(Ann:　Why did you take your umbrella this morning? It said on the radio that it was going to be a sunny day.)

　　Ann:　You _needn't have taken_ your umbrella this morning.

1　(Vicky:　Why did you go to the electricity office to pay the bill yesterday? This letter says you can pay with a cheque in the post.)

　　Vicky:　You _____ to the electricity office yesterday.

2　(Bill:　You don't need to phone Sarah. I'll invite her to the party tomorrow.)

　　Bill:　You _____ Sarah. I'll invite her to the party tomorrow.

3　(Susan:　It wasn't necessary to buy more food. John and Mary have just phoned to say that they can't come for dinner.)

　　Susan:　I _____ more food. John and Mary can't come for dinner.

4　(Peter:　Why did you work during the weekend? We don't have to finish this before Friday.)

　　Peter:　You _____ during the weekend.

5　(Bob:　You don't need to pay the whole amount now. You can pay some now and pay the rest later.)

　　Bob:　You _____ the whole amount now.

23 Should, ought to, had better

1 We use **should**, **ought to**, and **had better** with an infinitive (e.g. **be**, **go**, **ask**, **wait**):

	INFINITIVE
I should	*go.*
You ought to	*ask.*
We had better	*wait.*

2 We use both **should** and **ought to** to ask for or to give advice, to say what is the correct or best thing to do:

A: *I've got toothache. What **should** I **do**?*
   (= What is the best thing for me to do?)
B: *You **should go** to the dentist's.*
   (= The best thing for you to do is to go to the dentist's.)

When we are talking about a duty or a law, we usually use **ought to**:

A: *I saw a robbery. What **should** I **do**?*
B: *You **ought to report** it to the police.*
   (= It is a person's duty to report it.)

On the other hand, when we are giving a personal opinion, we usually use **should**:

B: *I think you **should forget** about it.*

We use **should** much more than **ought to** in negatives and questions:

*I **shouldn't** go.* (or *I **ought not to** go.*)
Should I go? (or *Ought I to go?*)

3 We can also use **had better** to give advice, to say what is the best thing to do:

The train is going to leave now. You'd better get on it.

*There'll be a lot of traffic tomorrow. We **had** (or We'**d**) **better leave** early.*
*I **had** (or I'**d**) **better ask** the doctor about the pain in my stomach.*

Note that **had** is a past form, but it does not refer to past time here; we use it to talk about present or future time.

We only use **had better** to give advice about a particular thing; when we give general advice, we use **should** or **ought to**:

*When people are in trouble, they **should go** to the police. (Not …they had better go to the police.)*

The negative is **had better not**:
*They **had better not be** late.*

....

Practice

A **Put in the right form of the verbs in the box.**

start	~~tell~~	have	listen	try	wait

0 They ought _to tell_ the manager about this problem.
1 Should we _____ to phone them again?
2 They had better _____ the work at once.
3 We shouldn't _____ to what they say.
4 It's a bit windy. We'd better _____ lunch here in the house, not outside in the garden.
5 We ought _____ until the police arrive.

B **Make these sentences negative by putting *not* in the right place.**

0 Henry should stay in bed. _Henry shouldn't stay in bed today._
1 You ought to move it. _____
2 They had better come after supper. _____

3   We should change everything. _____

4   You'd better tell the director. _____

C   **Use *should* or *shouldn't* and one of the phrases from the box in each dialogue.**

call an ambulance	give you a new cup
drive home in her car	leave everything where it is
~~decide for herself~~	move the person yourself
borrow money	~~do anything about it~~
let him eat so much	make him do lots of sport
~~report it to the police~~	ask someone to take her
touch anything	

0   A: There is a house near my home where I often hear a child crying.

B: You _should report it to the police_ .

0   A: My daughter wants to marry a sailor. What should I do about it?

B: In my opinion, _you shouldn't do anything about it_ . Your daughter
should decide for herself .

1   A: If someone has a serious accident, what's the right thing to do?

B: Well, you _____ . It's not a good idea to move an
injured person. Instead, you _____ to take the person
to hospital.

2   A: Last Saturday I bought some coffee cups but one of the handles was broken. What can I
expect the shop to do?

B: They _____ .

3   A: My son is 12 years old and he's already very fat.

B: Well, it's important not to eat too much, so you _____ .
Also, you _____ .

4   A: If you come home and see that you've been robbed, what's the best thing to do?

B: Well, you _____ . You
_____ and call the police.

5   A: Mary can't work because she's feeling sick. How can she get home?

B: Well, she _____ . She
_____ home.

6   People _____ if they can't pay it back.

D   **Use the sentences in brackets to write a reply with *had better* in the following dialogues.**

0   A: I've got a headache.

B: (You should go and lie down.) _You'd better go and lie down_ .

1   A: The children want to play in the kitchen.

B: (Well, they should clear everything away when they finish.) Well,
_____ when they finish.

2   A: I think it's going to rain.

B: (Yes, we ought to take our umbrellas.)   Yes, _____ .

3   A: I'm going to go to bed now. We have to get up very early tomorrow.

B: (Yes, I should go to bed early too.)   Yes, _____ .

24 Had to go, should have gone

1 Look at this example:

*Jane **had to wait** an hour for a bus.*
Had to wait means that Jane waited because no bus came for an hour.

We use **had to** to talk about something that someone did because it was necessary.

If someone did not do something because it was not necessary, we use **didn't have to**:
*I **didn't have to work** last Saturday.*
(= I didn't work because it was not necessary.)
The question form is **did…have to**:
***Did** you **have to work** last Saturday?*

2 Now consider this situation:

> Pam's job includes working on Saturday. Last Saturday she was ill, so she didn't work:
> *Pam **should have gone** to work last Saturday, but she was ill. So she stayed at home.*

We use **should have** (**done/gone** etc.) to say that something which did not happen was the correct or best action. We can also use **should have** to criticize someone. Look at this example:

> Peter, a farm worker, didn't close a gate, and the cows got into the wrong field:
> *Peter **should have closed** the gate.*

We use **shouldn't have** (**done/gone** etc.) to say that something which did happen was not the correct action:
*I **shouldn't have got** angry with Jane.*
(= I got angry with Jane, but it was not a good thing to do.)
*Peter **shouldn't have left** the gate open.*

Practice

A Complete the dialogues with *had to*, or *did…have to* and the words in brackets.

0   Jim: When you had that stomach trouble, <u>did you have to</u> (you) go into hospital?

    Joan: No, I <u>didn't have to</u> (not) go into hospital, but I <u>had to</u> stay in bed for a week.

1   Alan: Was there a translation in the exam?

    Jane: No, we _____ (not) translate anything, but we _____ write three essays.

2   Ann: I was very busy yesterday.

    Bill: What _____ (you) do?

    Ann: I _____ prepare everything for today's meeting.

3   Ken: _____ (you) wear uniform when you were at school?

    Jean: Yes, and we _____ make sure it was always neat and tidy, as well.

4   Tom: What _____ (you) do to get your international driving licence?

    Tina: I _____ show the police my national driving licence, but I _____ (not) take another driving test.

5   Mark: Our children enjoyed their holiday at the summer camp.

       Mary: _____ (they) help at mealtimes?

       Mark: Well, they _____ (not) make the food, but they

                _____ help with the washing-up.

B   Complete the sentences with *should have* or *shouldn't have* for these situations.

0   Philip didn't take his medicine. Later he got very ill.

     Philip <u> should have taken </u> his medicine.

0   Sara drove her car when she was tired and she had an accident.

     Sara <u> shouldn't have driven </u> her car when she was tired.

1   Tony didn't buy any sugar so he couldn't make a cake.

     Tony _____ some sugar.

2   Sally had a cold but she still went to the cinema. Later she had to stay in bed.

     Sally _____ to the cinema.

3   Ted ate a lot of apples. Later he had stomach ache.

     Ted _____ so many apples.

4   Lucy didn't lock the door to her flat when she went to buy a newspaper. While she was away, someone stole her television.

     Lucy _____ the door when she went out.

5   Mary borrowed Tom's camera without asking him.

     Mary _____ Tom's camera without asking him.

C   Here is the work plan for the Information Office at Heathrow Airport for last weekend. If someone did not in fact work, there is a comment.

SATURDAY		SUNDAY	
On duty	Comments	On duty	Comments
Jenny	✓	Colin	✓
Brian	ill	Mary	✓
Joan	ill	Derek	ill
Daniel	✓	Carol	ill

From the information in the table, write complete sentences using *had to*, *didn't have to*, or *should have* and the words in brackets.

0   (Jenny/Saturday)   <u>Jenny had to work on Saturday.</u>

0   (Colin/Saturday)   <u>Colin didn't have to work on Saturday.</u>

0   (Carol/Sunday)   <u>Carol should have worked on Sunday</u> but she was ill.

1   (Colin/Sunday)   _____

2   (Joan/Sunday)   _____

3   (Derek/Sunday)   _____ but he was ill.

4   (Mary/Saturday)   _____

5   (Brian/Saturday)   _____ but he was ill.

6   (Daniel/Saturday)   _____

7   (Joan/Saturday)   _____ but she was ill.

8   (Derek/Saturday)   _____

25 Passive sentences (1) (**It is made**)

1 These two sentences describe the same event:

ACTIVE: *Ann took* | OBJECT *these photos.* |

PASSIVE: | *These photos* | *were taken by Ann.* SUBJECT

The object (**these photos**) in the active sentence corresponds to the subject in the passive sentence. The subject (**Ann**) in the active sentence corresponds to the phrase with **by** in the passive sentence (**by Ann**).

2 Here are some passive tenses:

	SUBJECT + **be** + PAST PARTICIPLE
Present Simple:	**it is taken, they are taken**
Past Simple:	**it was taken, they were taken**
Present Perfect:	**it has been taken, they have been taken**
will (Future):	**it will be taken, they will be taken**

3 We use the passive when we do not know who did the action or when it is not important to say who did it:
*Our car **was made** in Korea.*
*The work **will be finished** today.*

We also use the passive to make the topic of a conversation into the subject of the sentence. For example, if a dog bit a girl, we can say:
A: *What did the dog do?* (topic: the dog)
B: *It **bit** the girl.* (active)
Or:
A: *What happened to the girl?* (topic: the girl)
B: *She **was bitten** by a dog.* (passive)

3 Some verbs, like **give**, have two objects:

	OBJECTS	
	+person	+thing
ACTIVE: *They gave*	*Diana*	*a camera.*

We usually make the person (e.g. **Diana**) the subject of a passive sentence:
PASSIVE: *Diana was given a camera.*

Other verbs that can have two objects are:

ask	pay	sell	offer	tell
bring	send	lend	promise	

....

Practice

A Write complete sentences from the words in brackets. Use the Past Simple passive.

0 (St. Paul's Cathedral/complete/ in 1710) _St. Paul's Cathedral was completed in 1710._

0 (Millions of Beatles records/sell/in the 1960s) _Millions of Beatles records were sold in the 1960s._

1 (The planet Pluto/discover/in 1930) _____

2 (Two atomic bombs/drop/on Japan in 1945) _____

3 (John F. Kennedy/kill/in Dallas) _____

4 (The first Apple computers/produce/in the 1970s) _____

5 (The Eiffel Tower/build/a hundred years ago) _____

6 (The first jet planes/make/in Germany) _____

7 (The Taj Mahal/build/in the 17th century) _____

8 (In 1957, millions of pounds/steal/from a train) _____

9 (Queen Elizabeth/crown/in 1953) _____

10 (In the old days, horses/use/for transport) _____

11 (The first books/print/in the 15th century) _____

12 (Everest/climb/for the first time in 1953) _____

B Each of the following sentences tells us something about a person. Express the same fact in a sentence that tells us about the thing and that has a passive verb. Use *by*.

0 Picasso painted 'Guernica'.
   'Guernica' was painted by Picasso.

1 Alexander Fleming discovered the drug penicillin.
   _____

2 The Beatles wrote the song 'Yesterday'.
   _____

3 Agatha Christie created the detective Hercule Poirot.
   _____

4 Beethoven composed the 'Eroica' symphony.
   _____

5 Margaret Mitchell wrote 'Gone with the Wind'.
   _____

6 Alexander Bell invented the telephone.
   _____

7 Frank Whittle designed the jet engine.
   _____

8 Steven Spielberg directed 'Jurassic Park'.
   _____

9 Leonardo da Vinci painted the 'Mona Lisa'.
   _____

C Use a passive sentence to say the same as the sentence in brackets, but do not say who did the action. Use the correct tense.

0 They asked John a lot of difficult questions.
   John _was asked a lot of difficult questions._

1 They gave Mary some flowers.
   Mary _____

2 They offered Jane a wonderful job.
   Jane _____

3 He will give all the children a present.
   All the children _____

4 Somebody sent me a strange letter.
   I _____

5 They will pay Mrs Jenkins over five hundred pounds.
   Mrs Jenkins _____

6 Her parents have promised Ann a bicycle for her birthday.
   Ann _____

7 They gave Madame Curie the Nobel Prize for Chemistry in 1911.
   Madame Curie _____

8 They didn't tell us the truth.
   _____

26 Passive sentences (2)

1 Here is a summary of passive tenses. Note that we always use a past participle in a passive verb (e.g. **typed**, **taken**). For more information on past participles, see Tables E and F on page 96.

Present Simple:

	VERB (present) + PARTICIPLE
ACTIVE:	Someone **types** the letters.
PASSIVE:	The letters **are** typed.

Past Simple:

	VERB (past) + PARTICIPLE
ACTIVE:	Someone **took** my camera.
PASSIVE:	My camera **was** taken.

Present Perfect:

	have/has + PARTICIPLE + PARTICIPLE
ACTIVE:	She **has packed** the books.
PASSIVE:	The books **have been** packed.

Past Perfect:

	had + PARTICIPLE + PARTICIPLE
ACTIVE:	Bob **had paid** the bill.
PASSIVE:	The bill **had been** paid.

Present Continuous:

	am/is/are + -ing + PARTICIPLE
ACTIVE:	They **are mending** the car.
PASSIVE:	The car is **being** mended.

Past Continuous:

	was/were + -ing + PARTICIPLE
ACTIVE:	They **were building** it.
PASSIVE:	It **was being** built.

will, can, must etc:

	will etc. + INFINITIVE + PARTICIPLE
ACTIVE:	We **will finish** the job.
PASSIVE:	The job **will be** finished.
ACTIVE:	We **must do** the work.
PASSIVE:	The work **must be** done.

2 In all passive sentences, the first verb (= auxiliary verb) is singular if the subject is singular, and plural if the subject is plural:

	AUXILIARY VERB	
The house	**is**	being built.
The houses	**are**	being built.

We also use the auxiliary verb to make questions and negatives:
Have the books been packed?
The bill **hadn't** been paid.

Practice

A Complete the sentences with a passive form of the verb in brackets.

0 Bread _is made_____ (make) from flour.

0 I was at school when these houses _were being built_____ (was building).

1 Cakes _____ (make) from flour.

2 We lived in a caravan in the garden while our house _____ (was building).

3 These letters _____ (must type) before 5 o'clock.

4 All the windows _____ (have cleaned) this week.

5 These cups _____ (broke) when we arrived.

6 Some money _____ (have stolen) from Tom's jacket.

B **Make questions from the passive sentences in brackets.**

0 (That car was made in Germany.) Where <u>was that car made?</u>

1 (Mary was examined by the doctor this morning.) When _____

2 (The food will be prepared on Friday.) When _____

3 (This window has been broken three times.) How many times _____

C **Write the negative of the sentences in exercise B.**

0 That car <u>was not made in Germany.</u>

1 Mary _____

2 The food _____

3 This window _____

D **Make these active sentences passive. Use a phrase with *by*.**

0 Your manager must write the report.

The report <u>must be written by your manager.</u>

0 The children are organizing the Christmas party.

The Christmas party <u>is being organized by the children.</u>

1 The French team has won the silver medal.

The silver medal _____

2 A woman was training the guard dogs.

The guard dogs _____

3 People of all ages can play this game.

This game _____

4 A large crowd was watching the match.

The match _____

5 The secretary sent a reply.

A reply _____

6 Two different teachers have marked the exams.

The exams _____

7 A police car is following that green van.

That green van _____

E **Complete the sentences with the correct passive form of the verb in brackets.**

0 The castle <u>was built</u> (build) in 1546.

0 These mountains can <u>be seen</u> (see) from a great distance.

1 These houses _____ (build) in 1946.

2 The repairs must _____ (finish) by tomorrow.

3 The town has _____ (attack) several times since the beginning of the war.

4 The decision has already _____ (take).

5 The letters will _____ (post) tomorrow morning.

6 White wine can _____ (make) from red grapes.

7 The accident happened while the cars _____ (load) onto the lorries.

8 The letters _____ (type) at this very moment.

27 Have something done (We had it cleaned)

1 Look at this sentence:

▷ *Mary and Tim **painted** their flat.*
This tells us that Mary and Tim were the painters; they painted their flat.

Now look at this sentence with **have something done**:

▶ *Jenny and John **had** their flat **painted**.*
This tells us that Jenny and John wanted their flat painted, and that someone painted it for them.

2 Here are some more examples:

TENSE	+ OBJECT	+ PARTICIPLE
▷ I **have mended**	my bike.	
▶ I **have had**	my bike	**mended**.

▷ *Sheila **is going to cut** her hair.*
▶ *Sheila **is going to have** her hair **cut**.*
(= Someone is going to cut it for her.)

▷ *She **washes** her car every Sunday.*
▶ *She **has** her car **washed** every Sunday.*
(= Someone washes her car for her.)

▷ *I **must clean** my suit this week.*
▶ *I **must have** my suit **cleaned** this week.*
(= I must pay someone to clean it for me.)

▷ *I'll **mend** that broken window.*
▶ *I'll **have** that broken window **mended**.*
(= Someone will mend that window for me.)

3 We sometimes use **get** instead of **have**:
*I must **get** my suit **cleaned**.*

4 Now look at this example:

*Susan is very cross. She **had** her bike **stolen**.*
Here, we use **have something done** to talk about something that happens to someone, usually something unpleasant. Here is another example:
*The group **had** two concerts **cancelled** because of bad weather.*

....

Practice

A Make sentences with a form of *have something done* for these situations. Use the correct tense.

0 Tom's windows were dirty, but he didn't have time to clean them himself.
Last Saturday, Tom <u>had his windows cleaned.</u>

1 The shop delivers Mary's food to her house.
Mary _____

2 At the butcher's Fred said, 'Please cut the meat into small pieces'
Fred _____ into small pieces.

3 The hairdresser cuts Rachel's hair about twice a year.
Rachel _____ about twice a year.

4 Last week, the optician checked Mr Stone's eyes.
Last week, Mr Stone _____

5 Mrs Frost's doctor says to her: 'When you come to see me next week, I'll check your blood pressure.'
When Mrs Frost goes to see the doctor next week, she _____

6 Last week, the garage serviced Jane's car.
Last week, Jane _____

7 A builder is going to replace the gutters on our house.
We _____ on our house.

B Look at these signs from some shops and a garage. Then write what people think when they see the signs using the words in brackets and *have* or *had*.

0 WE REPAIR ALL KINDS OF BOOTS AND SHOES.

(That reminds me. I/must/my brown boots/repair)

That reminds me. _I must have my brown boots repaired._

1 LET US CLEAN YOUR CARPETS AND CURTAINS.

(My parents use that company. They/their carpets/clean/there)

My parents use that company. _____

2 CAN WE CHECK YOUR OIL AND TYRES?

(That reminds me. I/must/the tyres/check)

That reminds me. _____

3 WE MAKE KEYS OF ALL TYPES.

(I'd almost forgotten. I/ought to/a new key/make/for the front door)

I'd almost forgotten. _____

4 OUR SPECIALITY: PAINTING HOUSES AND FLATS.

(I don't think I can afford to/our flat/paint)

I don't think I can afford to _____

5 WE MEND WATCHES AND CLOCKS.

(That shop isn't expensive. I/my watch/mend/there last week)

That shop isn't expensive. _____

6 WE TEST YOUR EYES FREE

(Ah, yes! My husband/his eyes/test/there last winter)

Ah, yes! _____

7 WE REMOVE ALL KINDS OF STAINS FROM ALL KINDS OF CLOTHES.

(Wonderful! I'll take my suit there and/that coffee stain/remove)

Wonderful! I'll take my suit there and I'll _____

C Some unpleasant things happened to these people last week. Use the sentence in brackets to write a sentence with *had something done*.

0 (Mary's bag was pulled off her shoulder.)

Mary _had her bag pulled off her shoulder._

1 (Peter's driving licence was taken away by the police.)

Peter _____

2 (Paula's bike was stolen from the garage.)

Paula _____

3 (Fiona's glasses were broken.)

_____

4 (John's clothes were torn in a fight.)

_____

5 (Jane's flat was burgled at the weekend.)

_____

6 (Our electricity was cut off because we had forgotten to pay the bill.)

_____

28 Verb + to (He wants to help) or verb + -ing (I enjoy reading)

1 Look at these sentences:
> My sister **promised to help** me.
> John doesn't **want to wait**.

We use **to** + infinitive after these verbs:

afford	dare	decide	
deserve	want	hope	**+ to +**
learn	mean	offer	INFINITIVE
pretend	promise	refuse	
seem	have (='must')		

2 Look at these sentences:
> Have they **finished painting** the garage?
> We **enjoy sitting** in the garden.

We use an **-ing** form after these verbs:

avoid	dislike	enjoy	
finish	give up	imagine	**+ -ing**
keep	practise	stop	

3 Look at these sentences:
> Jenny **likes to stay** at home.
> Jenny **likes staying** at home.

These verbs can usually take an **-ing** form or **to** + infinitive with no difference in meaning:

begin	continue	hate	intend
like	love	prefer	start

But after **would hate, would like, would love** or **would prefer**, we use **to** + infinitive:
> **Would** you like to go for a walk?
> I'd **love to visit** Australia.

4 We can use an an **-ing** form or **to** + infinitive after these verbs, but the meaning is different:

try	remember	forget

▶ I **tried to lift** that heavy stone. (= make an attempt: I made an attempt to lift the stone.)
If you can't read where you are, **try sitting** nearer the window. (= test something out: Sit nearer the window and see if you can read there.)

▶ **Remember to go** to the bank. (= Remember that you must go to the bank.)
She **remembers going** to the bank. (= She remembers that she went to the bank.)

▶ Don't **forget to phone** Mrs Grey. (= Remember that you must phone Mrs Grey.)
I'll never **forget seeing** that rainbow. (= I saw that rainbow, and I'll always remember it.)

....

Practice

A Put in the correct form of the verb in brackets.

0   Paul dared _to argue_ (argue) with the police.

0   I can't imagine _living_ (live) in the country.

1   We've decided _____ (go) to the beach.

2   I stopped _____ (play) tennis when I got married.

3   I meant _____ (buy) some butter, but I forgot.

4   Did you promise _____ (take) the children to the zoo?

5   Have the men finished _____ (repair) the roof yet?

6   I'd love _____ (visit) China.

7   You shouldn't avoid _____ (talk) about your problems.

8   Peter refused _____ (help) us.

9   Would you prefer _____ (pay) now or later?

10   I couldn't afford _____ (live) in London.

11   Why does Peter keep _____ (talk) about his mother?

12   John hopes _____ (go) to China next year.

B   Complete this conversation between Janet and Sharon with the correct form of the verbs in brackets.

Janet: What do your children ⁰ _want to do_____ (want/ do) when they leave school?

Sharon: Well, Ann ⁰ _enjoys writing_____ (enjoy/ write), so she's
          ⁰ _hoping to work_____ (hope/work) for a newspaper. But I don't know about
          Paul. He ¹_____ (give up/ study) months ago. He seems to
          ²_____ (enjoy/ do) nothing now. He doesn't
          ³_____ (deserve/ pass) his exams. And he
          ⁴_____ (refuse/ listen) to us, when we tell him to
          ⁵_____ (keep/ study).

Janet: With our children, in the past, if we ⁶_____ (offer/ help) them,
          they always ⁷_____ (promise/ study) hard. Nowadays if they
          ⁸_____ (want/ talk) to us, that's fine, but I've learnt to
          ⁹_____ (stop/ ask) them questions. I suppose they
          ¹⁰_____ (dislike/ listen) to my suggestions. They
          ¹¹_____ (seem/ think) that they don't
          ¹²_____ (need/ study) hard , but one day they'll
          ¹³_____ (have/ find) a job.

C   Use an -ing form, or to + infinitive, of the word in brackets to complete each sentence.

0   You say that I've met Janet, but I can't remember her.
    I can't remember _meeting_____ (meet) Janet.

1   Please remember that you must buy some stamps.
    Please remember _____ (buy) some stamps.

2   We wanted to open the door, but we couldn't.
    We tried _____ (open) the door.

3   John met Madonna once. He'll never forget it.
    John will never forget _____ (meet) Madonna.

4   Sheila intended to phone Peter, but she forgot.
    Sheila forgot _____ (phone) Peter.

5   Jenny had a headache. She took an aspirin, but it didn't help.
    Jenny tried _____ (take) an aspirin for her headache.

6   I have a special soap that will probably get your hands clean.
    Try _____ (wash) your hands with this special soap.

7   It will not be easy to do all the work today.
    We'll try _____ (finish) the work before tonight.

8   I stayed in Jane's flat while she was on holiday. I remembered that I had to feed her cats every day.
    I remembered _____ (feed) Jane's cats every day while she was on holiday.

9   Remember that you must invite Mary to the party next week.
    Don't forget _____ (invite) Mary to the party next week.

29 Purpose: What is it for? ~ It's for cutting cloth.

1 Look at this dialogue:
A: *What's this machine for?*
B: *It's for cutting cloth.*
The question **What is it for?** asks about the purpose of something (what we use something for). When we describe the purpose of a thing, we use **for + -ing.** Here are some more examples:
This is an instrument for measuring wind speed.
This tool is used for making holes.

2 Now look at this dialogue:
A: *What does he need my camera for?*
(= Why does he need my camera?)
B: *He needs it for his work.* (= His work is the reason why he needs the camera.)
The question **What…for?** asks about purpose. To talk about someone's purpose, we can use **for + noun.** Here are some more examples:
A: *What did he go to the shops for?*
B: *He went to the shops for some fruit.*
(He wanted to buy some fruit.)

I buy the newspaper for the sports news.
(= …in order to read the sports news.)

3 Now look at this dialogue:
A: *What does he need my camera for?*
B: *He needs it to take some photos.* (= …in order to take some photos.)
To talk about someone's purpose, we can also use **to + infinitive** (e.g. **to take**). Here are some more examples:
He went to the shops to buy some fruit.
(= …in order to buy some fruit.)

John phoned the police to tell them about the burglar.

....

Practice

A Make definitions of the things in Box A using one of the phrases from Box B.

A		B
telescope — instrument		boil water
~~hammer — tool~~		measure temperature
fridge — appliance		~~knock in nails~~
kettle — appliance		clean carpets
thermometer — instrument		see things at a distance
vacuum cleaner — appliance		keep food cold
drill — tool		measure speed
speedometer — instrument		keep food frozen
freezer — appliance		make holes

0 A hammer <u>is a tool for knocking in nails.</u>

1 A kettle _____

2 A thermometer _____

3 A vacuum cleaner _____

4 A fridge _____

5 A telescope _____

6 A speedometer _____

7 A freezer _____

8 A drill _____

B In the following short dialogues, use *What ... for?* to make questions from the words in brackets. Then write a reply using the words in brackets and *for*.

0   A: (/ did/Tom/go/to the park/?)
    What did Tom go to the park for?

    B: (He/go/to the park/some fresh air)
    He went to the park for some fresh air.

1   A: (/ does/Mary/want/the money/?)
    _____

    B: (She/want /the money/a train ticket)
    _____

2   A: (/ does/Philip/want/the flour/?)
    _____

    B: (He/want/the flour/ a cake)
    _____

3   A: (/ did/Bill/go /to the butcher's/?)
    _____

    B: (He/go/to the butcher's/some sausages)
    _____

4   A: (/ does/Helen/want/the polish/?)
    _____

    B: (She/want/it/her shoes)
    _____

5   A: (/ did/Alison/go /to the library/?)
    _____

    B: (She/go/to the library/ a book on India)
    _____

6   A: (/ did/Jane/phone /Ann/?)
    _____

    B: (She/phone/Ann/some advice)
    _____

C Now write the answers from exercise B using one of the verbs in the box, as in the example. Use each verb once.

| borrow   buy (x2)   clean   get (x2)   make |

0   Tom: _He went to the park to get some fresh air._
1   Mary: _____
2   Philip: _____
3   Bill: _____
4   Helen: _____
5   Alison: _____
6   Jane: _____

30 Verb + object (+ to) + infinitive (I asked her to come)

1 Look at these examples:

> Carol said to Bob:
>   *'Make some coffee, please.'*
> We can say:
>   Carol **asked Bob to make** some coffee.

> Ann said to Rose:
>   *'Can you come to my party, Rose?'*
> We can say:
>   Ann **invited Rose to come** to her party.

> Tom thinks Chris should see a doctor. He
> can say:
>   *I'll* **persuade Chris to go** *to the doctor's.*

The structure is:

VERB	+OBJECT	+ to + INFINITIVE
She asked	*Jill*	*to wait.*
She asked	*her*	*to wait.*

We use these verbs in this structure:

tell	**force**	**teach**
help	**allow**	**remind**
ask	**invite**	**encourage**
want	**forbid**	**persuade**
advise	**would like**	

} + OBJECT + **to**

2 Note that the first verb can change its tense, but the second verb is always **to** + infinitive (**to make**):

> *She* **is asking Bob**
> *She* **will ask Bob** } **to make** *some coffee.*
> *She* **has asked Bob**

Note that if we use a pronoun, we use **me**, **him**, **us** etc. (object pronoun) after the verb:
> *Carol asked* **him** *to make some coffee.*

3 Now look at these two sentences:
> *The teacher* **let Jane leave** *school early.*
> *I* **made him tell** *me the truth.*

Let here means 'allow', and **make** means 'force' or 'order'. **Make** and **let** are followed by an infinitive (without **to**):

VERB	+ OBJECT	+ INFINITIVE
She	*let*	*Jane*	*leave.*

Feel, **hear**, **see** and **watch** can also be followed by an infinitive (without **to**):
> *I* **heard** *your sister* **shout** *'Fire!'* (Not ~~...to shout...~~)
> *Tom* **saw** *a car* **come** *round the corner.*

··

Practice

A   Write complete sentences from the words in brackets. Be careful to use the correct tense.

0   (Tomorrow/I/encourage/Janet/enter/the competition)

   Tomorrow I will encourage Janet to enter the competition.

0   (I was already tired, but I/force/myself/go on working)

   I was already tired, but I forced myself to go on working.

1   (Ann/teach/Mary/drive/last year)

   _____

2   (Don't worry! Tomorrow I/persuade/my father/see/a doctor)

   _____

3   (The boss has/forbid/his staff/wear/jeans in the office)

   _____

4   (Last Sunday, John/invite/Sheila/come/for lunch)

   _____

5   (Next year the teachers/allow/the students/use/calculators in exams)

   _____

B Use the words in brackets to complete the sentences.

   0 (Police: 'Can everyone please stay indoors?')
      The police asked everyone _to stay indoors._

   1 (Jane: 'Remember to come home early, Tim.')
      Jane reminded Tim _____

   2 (Manager: 'You must work quicker.')
      The boss wants us _____

   3 (Captain: 'Let's do our best in the game.')
      The captain encouraged us _____

   4 (Jane: 'Can you come to my party next Saturday?')
      Jane invited me _____

C Answer the questions, changing the nouns (e.g. *Michael*) to pronouns (e.g. *him*). Be careful to use the correct tense.

   0 A: Did Jane tell Michael to be careful?
      B: Yes, _she told him to be careful._

   1 A: Would Jane like Peter to stay?
      B: Yes, _____

   2 A: Did Mrs Slater help her son to finish?
      B: Yes, _____

   3 A: Did the doctor advise Michael to stay in bed?
      B: Yes, _____

   4 A: Does Susan allow her children to go to late-night parties?
      B: Yes, _____

   5 A: Did Mary remind Mark to phone?
      B: Yes, _____.

D Write a sentence with a similar meaning, using the verb in brackets.

   0 The police told everyone to leave the building.
      (make) _The police made everyone leave the building._

   1 The driver allowed the old man to travel on the bus without a ticket.
      (let) _____

   2 Jack told his younger brother to wash the dishes.
      (make) _____

   3 I don't allow people to smoke in my house or in my car!
      (let) _____

E Combine the two sentences into one.

   0 Your sister shouted 'Fire!' I heard her.
      I _heard your sister shout 'Fire!'_

   1 Tom prepared the sandwiches. Diane watched him.
      Diane _____

   2 The ground shook. We felt it.
      We _____

   3 Brian left early. Did you see him?
      Did you _____

31 What...like? (What's she like?)

1 Look at this question and answer:
A: *What's Julie like?*
B: *She's very pretty and she's very kind, but she's not very clever.*
We use **What...like?** to ask about a person's physical appearance (tall, short, pretty etc.) or character (interesting, boring, friendly, unfriendly etc).
We can also use **What...like?** to ask about places, books, films and events (e.g. a party, a football match):
A: *What's Rio de Janeiro like?*
B: *Well, the beaches are wonderful but the traffic is awful.*
A: *What's Spielberg's latest film like?*
B: *It's excellent.*

2 We use **look like?** to talk about someone's appearance:
A: *What does Julie look like?*
B: *She's tall with brown hair.*
We can also use **like** with **taste, feel, sound,** and **smell**:
A: *What does that taste like?*
B: *It tastes like cheese.*

A: *What is this material?*
B: *I don't know. It looks like wool but it feels like cotton.*

3 We can also use **like**, with the question word **Who** and in statements, to mean 'similar to':
A: *Who's Julie like—her father or her mother?*
B: *She's like her mother.* (= She is similar to her mother.)
Rio de Janeiro is like Buenos Aires. (= Rio is similar to Buenos Aires.)

4 The word **like** in **What's she like?** is a preposition; it is not the verb **like**. Here is an example of **like** used as a verb:
A: *What music does Julie like?*
B: *She likes rock music.*

5 We usually use **How?**, not **What...like?**, when we ask about someone's health or temporary state:
A: *How's your brother today?*
B: *He's feeling much better.*
A: *How was your boss today?*
B: *He was very friendly today!*

....

Practice

A Use the words in brackets to make a question that goes with the answer. Use *is /are* or **look**. Sometimes more than one answer is possible.

0 (What/Sally/like)
A: _What is Sally like_____ ? ~ B: She's clever, but she's a bit boring.

0 (What/Jane/like)
A: _What does Jane look like_____ ? ~ B: She's quite short and has dark hair.

1 (What/Peter/like)
A: _____ ? ~ B: He's not a very interesting person.

2 (What/Anna's parents/like)
A: _____ ? ~ B: They're very generous.

3 (What/Tom/like)
A: _____ ? ~ B: He's very tall, and he has blond hair.

4 (What/Eva/like)
A: _____ ? ~ B: She's tall and strong.

5 (What/Bob and Tom/like)
A: _____ ? ~ B: They're very amusing.

6 (What/Susan/like)
A: _____ ? ~ B: She's tall and slim, and she wears glasses.

B Read the following descriptions.

> Kiwis are a round, brown fruit with a rough skin. They have almost no smell, but they are sweet, with a flavour similar to strawberries.

> A double bass is a musical instrument. It is the largest member of the violin family. It has a deep sound.

Now for each of the answers, write a question about kiwis or a double bass, using *look/sound/taste/smell/feel* + *like*.

	QUESTION		ANSWER
0	What do kiwis look like	? ~	They're round and brown.
1	_____	? ~	It has a deep sound.
2	_____	? ~	They don't really have a smell.
3	_____	? ~	They have a flavour like strawberries.
4	_____	? ~	Like a very big violin.
5	_____	? ~	They are rough to the touch.

C Use the words in brackets to write a question with the preposition *like* or the verb *like*. Add any other necessary words.

0 (What music/you/like)
   A: What music do you like _____ ? ~ B: I like rock music.

0 (What/Julie/like)
0 A: What is Julie like _____ ? ~ B: She is very amusing.

1 (Who/your sister/like)
   A: _____ ? ~ B: She likes a boy in her class.

2 (What/Paul's brothers/like)
   A: _____ ? ~ B: They think they're clever, but I don't.

3 (What/Jane/like/for breakfast)
   A: _____ ? ~ B: She likes toast and marmalade

4 (Who/you/like)
   A: _____ ? ~ B: I'm like my mother.

5 (What/Mary's husband/like)
   A: _____ ? ~ B: He is rather boring. He's not like her.

6 (What sports/you/like)
   A: _____ ? ~ B: I like swimming and football.

D Write questions with *What…like?* (for things that are permanent) or *How…?* (for health or temporary situations). Use a form of *be* and the other words in brackets.

0 (be/Atlanta) What is Atlanta like _____ ? ~ It's a very modern city.
0 (be/Mike/yesterday) How was Mike yesterday _____ ? ~ He felt a lot better.
1 (be/John's flat) _____ ? ~ It's very big, and it has a wonderful view over the city.
2 (be/your boss/yesterday) _____ ? ~ He was tired but friendly.
3 (be/a squash racquet) _____ ? ~ It's similar to a tennis racquet, but lighter.
4 (be/your sister) _____ ? ~ She's very well, thank you.
5 (be/Portugal) _____ ? ~ It's very interesting. There are lots of things to see.

32 Questions and question words (**Who, What** etc.)

1 Questions to which we can reply 'yes' or 'no' have a form of **be** or an auxiliary (e.g. **can, have, do, would**) before the subject:

	SUBJECT	
Is	*Mary*	*here? ~ Yes, she is.*
Can	*Roger*	*swim? ~ No, he can't.*
Are	*they*	*going to leave? ~ Yes, soon.*
Has	*Simon*	*left yet? ~ No, he hasn't.*

2 If there is a question word (e.g. **Where, Who, What**), it goes before **be** or the auxiliary:

	SUBJECT	
Where is	*Mary*	*?*
What did	*Roger*	*do on Sunday?*
Where have	*they*	*gone?*

3 **Who** is for people. **What** is for things:
   Who did you meet yesterday? ~ I met Peter.
   What do you want for lunch? ~ Soup, please.
We use **Which** for a choice between a limited number of people or things. Compare **Which** and **What**:
   What sports do you like? ~ I like football and hockey.
   Which do you like best, football or hockey? ~ I like hockey best.

4 **Which** (but not **Who** or **What**) can have a phrase with **of** (e.g. **Which of them**):
   Which of these pictures did you paint?

5 Here are examples of other question words:
   Where do they live? ~ In Dublin.
   When do they get up? ~ At 7 o'clock.
   Why is Tom in bed? ~ He's got a headache.
   Whose car is that? ~ It's my mother's.
   How do you get to work? ~ By bus.
   How long did he stay? ~ One or two days.
   How far is it to York from here? ~ 20 miles.
We use **How many** with plural nouns and **How much** with uncountable nouns:
   How many records have you got? ~ About 40.
   How much milk do you want? ~ Two pints.
(For more details on uncountable nouns, see Table B, page 94.)

6 If the question word is the subject, then the word order is the same as in a statement:

SUBJECT	
Who	*took my pen? ~ Neil took it.*
What	*happened? ~ Nothing happened.*
Which of them	*won the race? ~ Sue won it.*
How many people	*came? ~ Twelve came.*

Practice

A Choose a suitable word from the box for each question, and put it in the right gap.

are	~~can~~	did	~~was~~	do	does	has	shall	who	you	what	is

0 __Was__ John __—__ at work last week?

0 Where __can__ I __—__ buy a stamp?

1 _____ Tim and Jenny _____ going to Oxford tomorrow?

2 _____ Philip _____ ever been on television?

3 How many photos _____ they _____ take yesterday?

4 Where _____ your sister _____ work?

5 _____ you _____ have _____ a shower every morning?

6 What _____ I _____ bring when I come to see you tomorrow?

7 _____ lives _____ in that big house across the street?

8 _____ did _____ Ted say to Bill?

9 Would _____ like _____ to come on holiday with us?

10 Where _____ Ann _____ living at the moment?

B Write the questions in the correct tense. Use the words in brackets and the question words in the box. Use any other words you need.

~~when~~   what (×2)   which   which of (×2)   who (×2)

0 (…leave/school) _When did you leave school_ ? ~ I left school last year.

0 (…these books/Sally/read) _Which of these books has Sally read_ ? ~ She has read all of them.

1 (…Jane/have /for breakfast) _____ ? ~ She has toast and coffee.

2 (…you/ see/at the station) _____ ? ~ I saw John.

3 (…Mary/prefer/ ,tea or coffee) _____ ? ~ She prefers tea.

4 (…you/studying/at university) _____ ? ~ I'm studying chemistry.

5 (…these two books/you/buy) _____ ? ~ I'm buying both of them.

6 (…they/invite/to their party) _____ ? ~ They're inviting all their friends.

C Use the 'full' answers to write questions with *Where, How much, When* etc. (We usually use the short, underlined answers when we reply to a question.)

QUESTION	ANSWER
0 _Where do Tom and Jean live_ ? ~	(Tom and Jean live) in Plymouth.
0 _How much butter have you bought_ ? ~	(I've bought) half a kilo of butter.
1 _____ ? ~	(Lucy is going to come) tomorrow.
2 _____ ? ~	(They borrowed) Maria's car.
3 _____ ? ~	(They've lived here) for four years.
4 _____ ? ~	(Michael has got) fifty compact discs.
5 _____ ? ~	(Pam goes to work) by bus.
6 _____ ? ~	(They stopped working) because the lights went out.
7 _____ ? ~	(That bicycle is) mine.
8 _____ ? ~	(The coast is) five miles (from here).

D Use the information in brackets to write a suitable question for each reply.

0 (Tina Taylor interviewed the winner.)

   a Who _did Tim Taylor interview_ ? ~ The winner.

   b Who _interviewed the winner_ ? ~ Tina Taylor.

1 (Jack is going to help Susan.)

   a Who _____ ? ~ He's going to help Susan.

   b Who _____ ? ~ Jack .

2 (John won three prizes.)

   a How many _____ ? ~ Three.

   b Who _____ ? ~ John.

3 (There are three machines; the machine in the corner makes the boxes.)

   a Which _____ ? ~ The one in the corner.

   b What _____ ? ~ It makes boxes.

4 (Mary ate Tim's sandwiches.)

   a Whose _____ ? ~ She ate Tim's sandwiches.

   b Who _____ ? ~ Mary did.

33 Reported speech (**She said that…**); **say** or **tell**

1 Look at this example:

> Mike: '*I've never been abroad.*'
> Mike **says** (that) he has never been abroad.

When we use a present tense reporting verb (e.g. **say/says**), the tense of the original verb does not change. We can use **that** after **say/says**, but we do not have to. We use **say/says** to report a conversation that we are still in the middle of:

2 When we report a statement later, then we usually use a past reporting verb (e.g. **said**), and we usually change the tense of the original verb:

A: *Where's Paul?*
B: *Oh, he said (that) he **was** ill.*

> Jean: '*I want to come to the party.*'
> Jean said (that) she **wanted** to come to the party.

3 The most common tense changes are:
- Present → Past: **am/is → was   are → were   go → went   is going → was going**
- Present Perfect → Past Perfect: **has taken → had taken**
- Past Simple → Past Perfect: **took → had taken**
- Modals: **will → would   can → could   may → might   must → had to**

4 In reported speech we often need to change nouns and pronouns. For example:

> '*Sara's brilliant,*' said Joe.
> Later Joe could say:
> *I said (that) **Sara** was brilliant.*
> Sara could say:
> ***Joe** said (that) **I** was brilliant.*

5 Note that we can:
- **say that**
- **say to someone that**
- **tell someone that**

Look at these examples:
Joe: '*You're brilliant, Sara.*'
Joe said (that) she was brilliant.
Joe said to Sara (that) she was brilliant.
Joe told Sara (that) she was brilliant.
Joe told her (that) she was brilliant.
We cannot **say someone that**, and we cannot **tell that**:
Not *Joe said Sara (that) she was brilliant.*
Not *Joe told (that) she was brilliant.*

....

Practice

A These people are saying these things. Report them, using *says that*.

0 Paul: 'Atlanta is a wonderful city.'
    Paul says that Atlanta is a wonderful city.

1 Ruth: 'I go joggging every morning.'
   Ruth _____

2 Anna: 'Jenny isn't studying for her exams.'

   _____

3 Andrew: 'I used to be really fat.'

   _____

4 Jim: 'I can't swim.'

   _____

B People made these statements. Report them, using *said.*

0 'Mary works in a bank,' Jane said.
   Jane said Mary worked in a bank.

1 'I'm staying with some friends,' Jim said.

2 'I've never been to Russia,' Mike said.

3 'Tom can't use a computer,' Ella said.

4 'Everybody must try to do their best,' Jill said.

5 'Jane may move to a new flat,' Rachel said.

6 'I'll stay at home on Sunday,' Bill said.

C People made these statements. Make different reports for different situations.

0 Norman said: 'Rosa, I love you.'
   Later, Rosa said to her sister: Norman said that he loved me.

0 Jenny said: 'I like your paintings, Peter.'
   Later, Jenny said to a friend: I said to Peter that I liked his paintings.

1 Anna said: 'You can rely on me, Tom.'
   Later, Tom said to his brother: Anna said that _____

2 Susan said: 'Jane, your mother has been very kind.'
   Later, Jane said to her mother: Susan said that _____

3 Mary said: 'Jenny is staying with me, Peter.'
   Later, Peter said to Jenny: Mary said that _____

4 Christina said: 'I'll help you with your homework, Angela.'
   Later, Christina said to a friend: I said to Angela that _____

5 The teacher said: 'Class! You're making too much noise.'
   Later, the pupils said to their parents: The teacher said that _____

6 Mark said: 'John may come to your party, Andrew.'
   Later, Andrew said to John: Mark said that _____

D Rewrite the sentences in brackets using *tell* instead of *say.*

0 (Norman said to Rosa that he would be late.) Norman told Rosa that he would be late.

1 (She said to him that she liked his paintings.) _____

2 (You said to me that you liked that film.) _____

3 (Tom said to Ann that he felt ill.) _____

4 (She said to Bill that she was leaving.) _____

5 (I said to you that I couldn't find it.) _____

6 (Mary said to him that she would send the letter.) _____

7 (We said to them that we would arrive at six.) _____

34 Reported requests, orders, and advice

1 REQUESTS

There are different ways to make a request, e.g:

Sarah: *'Please wait a minute, Tom.'*
Sarah: *'Will you wait a minute, please?'*
Sarah: *'Tom, could you wait a minute, please?'*

We can report all of these requests in the same way, using **asked**:

Sarah **asked** Tom to wait a minute.

We do not usually use **please** in a reported question.

2 ORDERS

There are different ways to give an order:

'Stand up, John.'
'You must work harder.'

We can report orders like this, using **told**:

He **told** John to stand up.
He **told** me to work harder.

3 ADVICE

We can give advice like this:

'You should get married, Peter.'
'You should stop smoking, Jane.'

We can report advice like this, using **advised**:

He ***advised*** Peter to get married.
He ***advised*** Jane to stop smoking.

3 In reported speech, we use **ask**, **tell**, and **advise** like this:

VERB	+ OBJECT	+ **to** + INFINITIVE
Sarah asked	Tom	to wait.
She told	him	to stand.
He advised	Jane	to stop smoking.

Here is a list of common verbs that we use in this structure:

advise	ask	tell	order
persuade	remind	forbid	warn

Examples:

I'll remind them to come early.
I advised them to go to the police.

We cannot use **say** in this structure:

She said (that) he should wait.
(Not *She said him to wait.*)

3 To report a negative request, order etc. (e.g. *'Don't laugh'*), we use **not** + **to** + infinitive:

VERB + OBJECT + **not** + **to** + INFINITIVE
*Sara told Tom **not to laugh**.*
*They warned Ian **not to borrow** money.*
*I reminded John **not to be** late.*

....

Practice

A Rewrite the sentences using an object + *to* + infinitive, as in the example.

0 'Make some coffee please, Bob.'

Carol asked <u>Bob to make some coffee.</u>

1 'You must do the homework soon, Jane.'

She told _____

2 'Remember to buy a map, Ann.'

He reminded _____

3 'You should see a doctor, Mrs Clark.'

He advised _____

4 'Keep all the windows closed, Bill.'

They warned _____

5 'Go home, Paul.'

Francis told _____

6 'Please stay for supper, Bob.'

I tried to persuade _____

B Report what these people said using the words in brackets. Use the Past Simple, as in the example.

0 Fred said, 'Anne, would you lend me five pounds, please?'

(ask) <u>Fred asked Anne to lend him five pounds.</u>

1 I said to John, 'Remember to phone Sally.'

(remind) _____

2 'You must wash your hands, children,' the teacher said.

(tell) _____

3 'Please play the guitar, Tom,' said Jane.

(try to persuade) _____

4 'Mary, please lend me your bicycle pump,' said Paul.

(ask) _____

5 She said, 'Children, stay away from the water.'

(warn) _____

6 'You should see a lawyer' the policeman said to Mark.

(advise) _____

7 'Alan, have a shower immediately,' she said.

(tell) _____

8 I said, 'Sally, remember to take an umbrella.'

(remind) _____

C Complete the conversations using the words in brackets. You will also need a pronoun (e.g. *me*, *him*, *them*) and the word *not*. Use the Past Simple, as in the example.

0 A: Did you tell the children to clean the car?

B: (Yes, but I/tell/to use too much water)

<u>Yes, but I told them not to use too much water.</u>

1 A: Did you ask Bill to come to the meeting?

B: (Yes, and I/tell /to be late)

_____

2 A: Did the doctor tell your sister to keep warm?

B: (Yes, and she/warn /to go outside the house)

_____

3 A: Did you ask Michael to post the letters?

B: (Yes, and I/tell /to forget the stamps)

_____

4 A: Did the manager tell the players to go to bed early?

B: (Yes, and he /warn /to eat late at night as well)

_____

5 A: Did the policeman advise everyone to stay indoors?

B: (Yes, and he/tell /to go near the windows)

_____

6 A: Did the dentist advise you to eat carefully?

B: (Yes, and she particularly/warn /to eat nuts)

_____

35 Reported questions (**She asked if...**)

1 'Yes/no' questions have a form of **be** (e.g. **is**, **are**) or an auxiliary verb (e.g. **can**, **do**, **have**) that goes before the subject:

	SUBJECT	
'**Are**	*they*	*English?'*
'**Can**	*John*	*type?'*

We report these questions with **ask if**:

	SUBJECT	
*She asked **if***	*they*	*were English.*
*She asked **if***	*John*	*could type.*

Or:
*She asked **whether** they were English.*
*She asked **whether** John could type.*
Note that in a reported question we do not put **be** or an auxiliary before the subject.

2 Many questions begin with a question word (**Who**, **What**, **Where** etc.):

	SUBJECT	
'**Where does**	*Ann*	*live?'*
'**Why has**	*Jane*	*gone?'*

We report these questions with **ask**:

	SUBJECT	
*They asked **where**	*Ann*	*lived.*
*She asked **why**	*Jane*	*had gone.*

3 We can also **ask someone something**:
*The manager asked **me** if I could type.*
*They asked **him** where Sarah lived.*

4 Note that when we report a question that somebody asked, we usually change the tense of the verb:
'**Can** John swim?'
*He asked if John **could** swim.*
The most common tense changes are:
▶ Present → Past: **am/is → was**
   are → were   is living → was living
   live → lived
▶ Present Perfect → Past Perfect: **has gone**
   → had gone
▶ Past Simple → Past Perfect: **arrived →**
   had arrived
▶ Modals: **will → would   can → could**

We often also change other words, for example:

'*Have **you** finished, Mike?'*
*She asked Mike if **he** had finished.*

5 We can use **wanted to know** and **wondered** instead of **asked**:
*She **wanted to know** if they were English.*
 (or *She **wanted to know** whether they....*)
*She **wondered** why Jane had gone.*

....

Practice

A Use the sentence in brackets to complete each sentence. End each sentence with a full stop (.) or a question mark (?).

0 (Did they come?)   She asked __if__ they came _._

1 (Do you speak English?)   They asked me _____ I spoke English____

2 (I wanted to know why he had taken my key.)   _____ did you take my key____

3 (How many people came to the party?) I asked _____ people came to the party____

4 (Does Ann work on Saturdays?)   I asked _____ Ann worked on Saturdays____

5 (Can we meet tomorrow?)   I asked _____ we could meet tomorrow____

6 (I asked what he had done.)   _____ has he done____

7 (Was Tom born in 1965 or 1966?)   I asked them _____ Tom was born____

8 (Why has Jane gone home?)   I wondered _____ Jane had gone home____

9 (Where do you go for your holidays?)   I wanted to know _____ they went for their holidays ____

10 (Is Bill coming to the party, Jane?)   I asked Jane _____ Bill was coming to the party____

11 (I asked him where he worked.)   _____ do you work ____

B   Use the words in brackets to write a question, and then complete the reported question.

0   (Where/have/Maria/go /?)

Question: _Where has Maria gone?_

Reported question: I asked _where Maria had gone._

1   (do/Jim/often/play/football/?)

Question: _____

Reported question: I wondered if _____

2   (What/have/the children/eat/?)

Question: _____

Reported question: She wanted to know _____

3   (Where/be/Mark /going/?)

Question: _____

Reported question: I asked _____

4   (When/be/the next bus /?)

Question: _____

Reported question: We wanted to know _____

5   (Have/Ann/see/this film/?)

Question: _____

Reported question: Tom asked _____

6   (How many/student/will/come /on the trip?)

Question: _____

Reported question: Sara wondered _____

C   Steven Ellis robbed a bank. The police believe that Alan Reeves helped him. A policeman asked Reeves these questions:

0 ~~How long have you been out of prison?~~	
1 Have you worked since then?	4 Do you know Steven Ellis?
2 Does your sister give you money?	5 How long have you known Steven?
3 Who else gives you money?	6 Have you seen Steven recently?

Later the policeman talked about the interview. Complete what he said, using the questions in the box.

0   I asked him _how long he had been out of prison_ , and he replied that he had left prison six months ago.

1   Then I asked him _____. He told me that he hadn't found a job.

2   I asked him _____, and he said she did give him some money, but not very much.

3   Then I asked him _____. He replied that nobody else did.

4   I asked him _____, and he said that he and Steven were friends.

5   So I asked him _____, and he said that he had known him for six years.

6   Then I asked him _____, and he said that he couldn't remember.

36 A/an, some, any or the

Jan 5/09

1 We use **a** and **an** with singular nouns. We use **a** before a consonant sound:
  a pear   a house   a university (u = 'you')
We use **an** before a vowel sound:
  an apple   an hour   an honest woman
We make the plural of these phrases with **some** or **any**:
  some/any pears   some/any apples
We also use **some** and **any** with uncountable nouns (see Table B, page 94):
  some /any bread   some /any information

2 We use **a/an** when we do not need to make clear which person or thing we are talking about:
  Yesterday I bought a blouse and a skirt.
  Have you ever seen a rainbow?
  A climber has died in Tibet.
Notice that we use **a/an** with professions:
  My mother is an architect.
  James is a doctor.
We also use **some** and **any** when we do not need to make clear which people or things we are talking about:
  I bought some shoes today.
  I didn't meet any nice people at the party.
  Did you buy any bread at the supermarket?

4 We use **the** with singular, plural and uncountable nouns:
  the girl   the girls   the information

5 We use **the** when it is obvious which person or thing we are talking about because:
  ▶ we have already mentioned it or something related to it:
    A: *I've bought a blouse and a skirt.*
    B: *What colour is the blouse?*
    We took our children to a circus. The clowns were very good.
  ▶ the situation makes it clear:
    The moon is bright tonight.
    Is the radio in the kitchen?
    Let's meet at the station.

6 We also use **the** when we make it clear which person or thing we mean with words that identify it:
  This is the skirt that I bought.
  Do you know the girls in this photo?

7 We do not use **the** with a noun and a number:
  Do Exercise 3 on page 29.
But we use **the** with **first, second** etc. + noun:
  Do the third exercise.

....

Practice

A Put *a* or *an* in the gaps.
  0 _An_ hour is _a_ long time.
  1 Take _____ umbrella if you're going for _____ walk.
  2 Would you prefer _____ orange or _____ banana?
  3 We saw _____ interesting TV programme about _____ woman who lives alone on _____ island.

B In each pair of sentences, one sentence needs *a/an*, and the other needs *the*. Put them in.
  0 'Mary' is _a_ girls' name.
     'Mike' is _the_ name my parents gave me.
  1 Batsford is _____ town where my uncle lives.
     Winchester is _____ town in the south of England.
  2 Trains don't stop here because _____ station is closed.
     Almost all towns have _____ railway station.
  3 My sister wants to make _____ programme about her favourite hobby.
     _____ TV programme that we saw last night was terrible.

4 If you don't know how to get somewhere, you should ask _____ policeman.

I know _____ police officer whose photo was in the paper.

5 A German family lives in _____ house next to ours.

My cousin can't find _____ house to buy anywhere.

6 _____ woman behind you is Ann's mother.

On the plane I was sitting next to _____ woman with beautiful, red hair.

C Put *a, an* or *the* in the dialogues.

0 A: Have Ann and Mark got any pets?

B: Yes, they've got _a_ dog and _a_ cat.

A: Does _the_ dog like _the_ cat?

1 A: I'm reading _____ interesting book.

B: Who's _____ author?

A: Jane Sinclair — you know, she's _____ woman who has her own show on TV.

2 A: Have you got _____ ruler that I can borrow?

B: I've got _____ plastic one and _____ wooden one. But _____ wooden one is broken.

A: Well, lend me _____ plastic one then, please.

3 A: We saw _____ wonderful film last weekend.

B: Who was _____ director?

A: Bob Pine. He's never made _____ film before.

4 A: Why is _____ earth hottest at _____ equator?

B: Because that is _____ part of _____ earth that is closest to _____ sun.

D Put *a, an, some* or *the* in the gaps.

Last Saturday we went for 0 _a_ walk in 0 _an_ area of Yorkshire where we had never been before. At about lunchtime, we came to 1 _____ village that wasn't on our map. It had 2 _____ pretty square with 3 _____ trees and 4 _____ old church. 5 _____ sun was very hot. There were 6 _____ people sitting under 7 _____ trees in 8 _____ square, and we asked them what 9 _____ village was called. They told us that they were strangers there, and that they didn't know 10 _____ name. 11 _____ woman heard what we were talking about. She came over to tell us that 12 _____ village was called Bridgend. She told us she had lived there since she was 13 _____ young girl, and that now she was 14 _____ grandmother.

E Write each sentence in a different way.

0 Do Exercise three. _Do the third exercise._

1 Turn to the fourth chapter. _____

2 Who knows the answer to the second question? _____

3 I have to do sentence two. _____

4 Now look at the second test. _____

37 There or it/they

1 Look at these sentences:

> *There is a big market near the river; it is very good for fruit and meat.*
> *There are two buses on Sunday; they both go to the station.*

We use **there is/are** when we talk about something for the first time in a conversation, and when we say where it is or when it is. We do not use **there** to talk about the same thing again; we use singular **it** (here meaning 'the big market') or plural **they** (here meaning 'the two buses'). Here are some more examples:

> *There are two schools here; they are both new.*
> *There's a good programme on Sunday; it gives all the sports news.*

2 We use **there** with different forms of **be**:

> *There weren't any compact discs 20 years ago.*
> A: *Have there been any problems this year?*
> B: *Yes, there have.*
> *There used to be a park here.* (= There was a park here but it isn't here now.)
> *There may be some eggs in the fridge.* (= It is possible that there are some eggs...)

3 We also use **there is/are** etc. to talk about the number of people or things in a place. Look at these questions and answers:

> A: *How many people were there at your party?*
> B: *There were about 12.* (Not ~~We were about 12.~~)
>
> A: *Are there many restaurants where you live?*
> B: *Yes, there must be 10 or more.* (Not ~~They must be 10.~~)

We can use **of us**, **of them** etc. after the number:

> *There were about 12 of us.*

4 For the weather, we use **it** with a verb or adjective, but **there** with a noun:

> **it** + verb: It *rained/snowed* a lot last winter.
> **it** + adjective: It was *foggy/sunny/windy/cloudy*.
> **there** + noun: There was a lot of *fog/cloud*.

5 Notice these examples with **it takes**:

> *It takes seven years to become a doctor.*
> A: *How long does it take to make bread?*
> B: *It takes several hours (to make bread).*

These sentences describe the time that is necessary to do something.

....

Practice

A Put in *there is*, *there are*, *it is* or *they are*.

0 __There are__ two cinemas in our town; __they are__ both near my flat.

1 _____ one train on Sundays; _____ an express train.

2 _____ two national holidays this month, and _____ both on a Friday.

3 _____ several trees in our garden, but _____ not very tall.

4 _____ a big lake in the park; _____ very deep.

B Use *there* and the words in the box to complete the sentences. Use each word in the box once.

have been	~~is~~	may be	used to be	was	will be

0 __There is__ an accident on this road almost every day.

1 Last year _____ a terrible fire at that factory.

2 Next Monday at 7 p.m. _____ a meeting of the committee.

3 When I was young, _____ a lot more cinemas than there are now.

4 Since 1900 _____ two world wars.

5 _____ a late-night bus, but I'm not sure if there is.

C Write answers to the questions using *there were... of* and the words in brackets.

0 A: How many people were there at your party?

   B: (20/us) <u>There were 20 of us.</u>

1 A: How many of you were there in the car?

   B: (five/us) _____

2 A: How many sailors were there in the boat?

   B: (six/them) _____

3 A: How many people were there at the supper?

   B: (twelve/us) _____

D Rewrite the sentences using the word in brackets and *it* or *there*.

0 There was a lot of snow last winter.

   (snowed a lot) <u>It snowed a lot last winter.</u>

0 It's quite cloudy this morning.

   (quite a lot of cloud) <u>There's quite a lot of cloud this morning.</u>

1 There was a lot of rain last night.

   (rained a lot) _____

2 It was quite foggy at the weekend.

   (quite a lot of fog) _____

3 There's a lot of cloud this morning.

   (very cloudy) _____

4 It rained quite a lot last week.

   (quite a lot of rain) _____

E Look at the times needed to prepare certain foods, then write a statement or a question and answer.

bake bread	- about 3 hours
~~prepare a salad~~	~~- about 10 minutes~~
cook a stew	- about 2 hours
cook an omelette	- a few minutes
~~boil an egg~~	~~- about 3 minutes~~
make tea	- about 5 minutes.
make a cake	- about an hour.

0 It <u>takes about three minutes to boil</u> _____ an egg.

0 A: How long <u>does it take to prepare</u> _____ a salad?

   B: <u>It takes about 10 minutes.</u>

1 It _____ an omelette.

2 A: How long _____ tea?

   B: _____

3 It _____ bread.

4 A: How long _____ stew?

   B: _____

5 It _____ a cake.

38 So or such (She's so clever)

We use **so** and **such** to intensify adjectives. Compare:

1

*Helen got all the answers right. She is **so** clever.* (= She is very clever.) We use **so** before adjectives that do not have a noun after them, and before adverbs:	*Helen got all the answers right. She is **such a** clever person.* (= She is a very clever person.) We use **such a/an** before an adjective + singular noun (e.g. **person**). We use **such** before a plural noun (e.g. **feet**) or an uncountable noun (e.g. **food**):

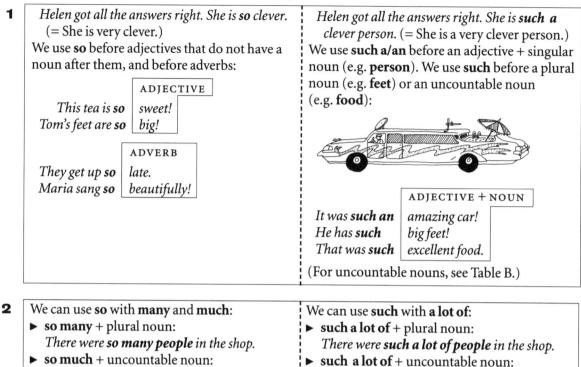

	ADJECTIVE
This tea is so	*sweet!*
Tom's feet are so	*big!*

	ADVERB
They get up so	*late.*
Maria sang so	*beautifully!*

	ADJECTIVE + NOUN
*It was **such an***	*amazing car!*
*He has **such***	*big feet!*
*That was **such***	*excellent food.*

(For uncountable nouns, see Table B.)

2

We can use **so** with **many** and **much**:	We can use **such** with **a lot of**:
▶ **so many** + plural noun: *There were **so many people** in the shop.*	▶ **such a lot of** + plural noun: *There were **such a lot of people** in the shop.*
▶ **so much** + uncountable noun: *We had so **much work** to do.*	▶ **such a lot of** + uncountable noun: *We had **such a lot of work** to do.*

3 Sentences with **so** and **such** can also describe the result of something:

	RESULT
*It was **so** dark*	*that we didn't see him.*
*He arrived **so** late,*	*he missed his plane.*

	RESULT
*It was **such a** dark night*	*that we didn't see him.*
*It was **such a** lovely day,*	*we went to the beach.*

Practice

A Put in *such* or *so*.

0 Tom is very handsome. He has <u>such</u> beautiful eyes.

0 It was a very pleasant trip because the guide was <u>so</u> nice .

1 My birthday was wonderful. I got _____ lovely presents.

2 It was difficult to drive because there was _____ much snow.

3 I like Tom. He is _____ a nice person.

4 We couldn't play tennis because it was _____ windy.

5 Jack loves his children. He is _____ a wonderful father.

6 Nobody listens to Jane because she says _____ silly things.

7 The nurses are wonderful here. They are _____ helpful.

8 Look at the stars. They are _____ bright tonight.

B Put *such*, *such a* or *such an* in the gaps.

0 Edinburgh is ___such a___ wonderful city.

1 Motorbikes are _____ dangerous machines.

2 I love skiing. It's _____ exciting sport. But it's a dangerous sport, too.

3 My cousin had _____ terrible accident. He almost died.

4 I like these new dresses. They have _____ pretty colours.

5 We had _____ wonderful meal. The food was excellent.

6 Susan Strange is _____ interesting writer.

C Use *so*, *such*, *such a* or *such an* to write sentences from the words in brackets. Put the verbs in the correct tense.

0 I can't believe that Tom is only thirteen. (He/have/grow/tall)
  He has grown so tall!

0 I never believe those boys. (They/be/always/tell/stupid lies)
  They are always telling such stupid lies!

1 I enjoy John's cooking. (He /be/wonderful cook)
  _____

2 I can't hear anything. (Those people /be/make /much noise)
  _____

3 Fred won three prizes. (He/be/lucky)
  _____

4 Sara always looks lovely. (She/ wear/pretty clothes)
  _____

5 We had three ice-creams. (They/be/delicious)
  _____

6 I don't smoke. (It/be/unhealthy habit)
  _____

7 I enjoyed that test. (It/be/easy)
  _____

D For each sentence, write another sentence with a similar meaning. Use *so…that*.

0 We decided not to phone them because it was very late.
  It was ___so late that we decided not to phone them.___

1 Sally didn't finish the exam because she worked very slowly.
  She worked _____

2 We didn't buy the camera because it was very expensive.
  The camera was _____

3 Paul didn't go out because he was very tired.
  Paul was _____

4 Peter couldn't see the holes because they were very small.
  The holes were _____

5 I couldn't finish the food because there was too much of it.
  There was _____

39 Adjective + preposition (**angry with**, **afraid of**)

1 Some adjectives can have a preposition + a noun (or pronoun) after them:

ADJECTIVE + PREPOSITION + NOUN			
I'm	*afraid*	*of*	*dogs.*
She's	*good*	*at*	*maths.*

Here are some more examples:
afraid of: *I'm **afraid of** my teacher.*
angry with: *John is very **angry with** me.*
annoyed with: *I was **annoyed with** my sister.*
brilliant at: *Jenny is **brilliant at** maths.*
busy with: *Tom was **busy with** his work.*
careless with: *Bill is **careless with** his money.*
cruel to: *Ann's mother was **cruel to** her.*
famous for: *France is **famous for** its cheese.*
fond of: *Peter is very **fond of** children.*
frightened of: *Our cat is **frightened of** your dog.*
full of: *The rooms were **full of** old furniture.*
good at: *Are you **good at** sport?*
grateful for: *They were **grateful for** our help.*
interested in: *She's **interested in** old coins.*
keen on: *He's very **keen on** chess.*
kind to: *Your sister was very **kind to** us.*
lucky at: *I'm often **lucky at** games.*

pleased with: *Ian was **pleased with** the result.*
proud of: *They're **proud of** their children.*
sure about: *Are you **sure about** her name?*
surprised by: *I was **surprised by** her anger.*

2 Some adjectives have a preposition + an **-ing** form after them:

ADJECTIVE + PREPOSITION + -ing FORM	
He was	*sick of washing*	dishes.

*I'm not very **good at running**.*
*Robert is very **fond of talking**.*
*Anne is **used to working** at night. (= She often works at night, and she doesn't mind it.)*

3 A few adjectives can have an **-ing** form without a preposition:

busy	no good	not worth

ADJECTIVE + -ing FORM	
They were	*busy getting*	things ready.

*It's **no good worrying** about the weather.*
*It's **not worth taking** the car; we can walk.*

....

Practice

A Put in the missing prepositions (e.g. *with*, *of*).

0 Mary was pleased __with__ her exam results. She had got good marks in most subjects.

1 Thank you very much. I am very grateful _____ your help.

2 I'm not sure _____ the price, but I think they cost about £5.

3 It was the day of the concert, and everyone was busy _____ the preparations.

4 I didn't expect to win the match. I was quite surprised _____ the result.

5 Sandra was very brave. We are very proud _____ her.

6 I like geography and I'm very interested _____ history as well.

7 We've got plenty of food. The fridge is full _____ things to eat.

8 Mary didn't like the director. She was annoyed _____ him.

9 John is very clever. He's brilliant _____ physics and chemistry.

10 Jane doesn't like small animals, but she's very fond _____ horses.

11 Jeff should look after his disks. He's very careless _____ them.

12 Susan and Jane like sports. They are particularly keen _____ hockey.

13 Colin must be good _____ French. He got top marks in the exams.

14 Mike has never learnt to swim because he's afraid _____ water.

B Write these short dialogues in the Present Simple. Use the words in brackets and any prepositions (e.g. *with, of, at*) that you need.

0 A: (Jane, why /be/you/angry/Peter?) ~ B: (Because he/be/very careless/his money)

A: ___Jane, why are you angry with Peter?___

B: ___Because he is very careless with his money.___

1 A: (be/ their daughter/good/school work?) ~ B: (Yes, in fact she/be/brilliant /everything)

A: _____

B: _____

2 A: (Why/be/Mr Bell's dog/afraid/him?) ~ B: (Because he/be/often/cruel/it)

A: _____

B: _____

3 A: (be/Jenny/fond/classical music?) ~ B: (Yes, she/be/very keen/Bach, for example)

A: _____

B: _____

4 A: (be/you/pleased/Peter's exam results?) ~ B: (Yes, we /be/ very proud/him)

A: _____

B: _____

C Use the words or phrases in the box to complete each sentence, and put in a preposition (e.g. *at, for*) if it is necessary.

talking to him	~~cards~~	listening to their problems
getting up early	its watches	old books

0 Maria has won again. She is usually lucky ___at cards___ .

1 I don't want to talk to them. I'm sick _____.

2 The boxes were heavy because they were full _____.

3 Alan never listens to anybody. It's no good _____.

4 I'm used _____ , but I know some people like to sleep late.

5 Switzerland is famous _____.

D Use the words in brackets to write complete sentences. Use the Present Simple. Add any necessary prepositions and make any necessary changes.

0 (Mrs Jackson/be/always/kind/me)

   ___Mrs Jackson is always kind to me.___

1 (It/be/not/worth/stay/until the end of the conference)

_____

2 (Mary/be/very good/make/people happy)

_____

3 (I/be /very interested/Jill's new ideas)

_____

4 (Tom/be/ busy/talk/to the guests)

_____

40 Prepositions (in, on, at, between, across etc.)

1 **In, on** and **at** are used to talk about places:
▶ We use **in** with enclosed spaces (e.g. rooms, buildings), and with limited areas (e.g. towns, parks, countries, continents):
  in *my pocket*   **in** *her car*   **in** *Germany*
▶ We use **on** with surfaces (e.g. walls, floors, shelves) and lines (e.g. paths, coasts, the equator):
  on *the grass*   **on** *the sea*   **on** *the line*
▶ We use **at** with a point (e.g. **at the bus stop**), and **at** with a building, when we mean either inside or outside:
  A: *Let's meet* **at** *the cinema.*
  B: *OK. Shall we meet* **in** *the cinema itself or* **on** *the pavement outside?*

Here are other prepositions of place:
  I sat **between** *Jane and Pam on the plane;*
  Ann was sitting **in front of** *me, and Carol was* **behind** *me.*
  Jane talked to the man **next to /beside** *her.*
  Buda lies **opposite** *Pest; together they are the city of Budapest.*
  We sat down to rest **under** *a large tree.*
  Please leave the flowers **outside** *my room.* (= not in my room)

2 **Into, onto,** and **to** are used to talk about movement:
  We moved the chairs **into** *my bedroom.*
  The actor ran **onto** *the stage.*
  They walked **to** *the next town.*

The opposites are **out of, off** and **from**:
  We moved the chairs **out of** *my bedroom.*
  The actor ran **off** *the stage.*
  We drove **from** *London to Edinburgh.*

Here are other prepositions of movement:
  They ran **across** *the field to the road.*
  Jim cycled **along** *the road to the next town.*
  I walked **up** *the hill and ran* **down** *the other side.*
  The bus went **past** *the bus stop without stopping.*
  The train goes **through** *three tunnels.*

3 **In, on** and **at** are also used to talk about time:
▶ We use **in** with years, seasons, and months:
  in *1987*   **in** *the spring*   **in** *May*
▶ Notice also: **in** *the morning/afternoon/ evening.*
▶ We use **on** with days and dates:
  on *Friday* **on** *Christmas Day* **on** *30th May*
▶ We use **at** for times:
  at *5 o'clock*   **at** *lunch-time*

....

Practice

A **Put *in, on* or *at* in the gaps.**

0 Peter lives __in__ Turkey.
1 There were some beautiful pictures _____ the walls of their sitting-room.
2 The children are playing _____ the grass _____ the park.
3 Does this bus stop _____ the railway station?
4 The books were _____ a box _____ a shelf _____ the garage.
5 Ecuador is _____ South America; it lies _____ the equator.
6 The gun was _____ the pocket of a dress that was hanging _____ the cupboard.

B **Look at this picture of a town, and complete the sentences.**

0 There is a road __beside__ the river.
1 There are some boats _____ the river.
2 The Town Hall is _____ the theatre.
3 The post office is _____ the theatre.
4 The theatre is _____ the Town Hall.
5 The post office is _____ the theatre and the police station.

C **Put the words in the box in the gaps.**

into (×3)	onto (×2)	~~to~~	out of	off

0   The march started in the park. From there we marched __to_____ the Town Hall.

1   The tiger escaped from its cage and jumped _____ the lake. It took a long time to get it _____ the lake and back _____ its cage.

2   Stupidly, Simon drove his car _____ the beach and then he couldn't move it, because the wheels sank _____ the sand. In the end he needed eight people to push it _____ the beach and back _____ the road.

D **Look at this picture of a town showing the route for a race.**

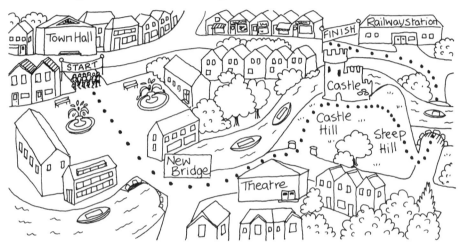

Now fill the gaps using the words in the box.

across	along	~~at~~	down	in front of
past	from	under	through	up

The race starts ⁰ __at_____ the Town Hall. The runners go ¹_____ the Town Hall and they run ²_____ the main square, to the river. Then they run over New Bridge and they go ³_____ the road beside the river for about 200 yards. They go ⁴_____ the theatre and ⁵_____ Castle Hill. They turn right ⁶_____ the Castle, and they go ⁷_____ Steep Hill. Then they go ⁸_____ the tunnel ⁹_____ the river, and they finish at the station.

E **Look at this page from a diary. Put in the information requested in the brackets. Use a preposition.**

April   1995
20   Monday
10 a.m Interview Kate Bell
in the London office
21   Tuesday

0   (the year?)   I interviewed Kate __in 1995._____

1   (the month?)   I interviewed Kate _____

2   (the date?)   I interviewed Kate _____

3   (the day?)   I interviewed Kate _____

4   (the part of the day?)   I interviewed Kate _____

5   (the time?)   I interviewed Kate _____

6   (the season?)   I interviewed Kate _____

41 Since, for, ago; first, last

1 **Since** is followed by a time (e.g. **6 o'clock**, **yesterday**), a year or date (e.g. **1945**), or an event (e.g. **the end of the war**):
> There **hasn't been** a world war **since 1945**.
> Things **have changed** a lot **since the end of the war**.

We use **since** to talk about a period from that time in the past to now:

| past | | (1945) | 1965 | 1985 | | now |

since 1945

Note that we use **since** with the Present Perfect (e.g. **have changed**). But a verb after **since** is about an event, and it must be in the Past Simple:
> Things have changed a lot **since** the war **ended**.

2 We use **for** with a period of time (e.g. **6 years**), to answer the question **How long?**:
> A: *How long did the war continue?*
> B: *The war continued **for 6 years**.*

| past | | 1 | 2 | 3 | 4 | 5 | 6 | | now |

for 6 years

The verb in the example is Past Simple (**continued**), but we can use **for** with other tenses to talk about a period of time in the present, the past, or the future:
> A: ***How long** is Mary staying?*
> B: *She**'s staying for five days**.*

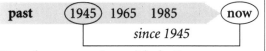

past	now	future
1	2	3	4	5

for five days

> There **hasn't been** a world war **for many years**.
> It **will** probably **snow for several hours**.

3 If we talk about the start and end of a period, we use **from** (not ~~since~~) and **to**:
> The war lasted **from** 1939 **to** 1945.

4 We can use **ago** with a Past Simple verb to say **when** something happened:
> A: ***When** did the Second World War start?*
> B: *It started over **50 years ago**.*
> (= It started 50 years back in the past from now.)

5 Look at these sentences, where **first** means 'for the first time' and **last** means 'for the last time':
> Jane and Bill **first met** 10 years ago.
> The planet Pluto **was first seen** in 1940.
> A: *When **did** you **last visit** Scotland?*
> B: *I **last visited** Scotland two years ago.*

Practice

A Put in **when, how long, ago, since, for** or **from** in the gaps.

0 ___When___ did you leave the office?

1 My mother died five years _____ .

2 I was at university _____ 1989 to 1993.

3 They've worked here _____ about five years.

4 We've lived here _____ 1989.

5 _____ did you start your present job?

6 _____ have you had your present job?

B Put the verbs in brackets in the gaps in the right form.

0 I __saw__ (see) Tony two or three days ago.

1 Nothing interesting _____ (happen) since my birthday.

2 Michelangelo _____ (live) from 1475 to 1564.

3 Marilyn Monroe _____ (die) over thirty years ago.

4 Marilyn Monroe _____ (be) dead for over thirty years.

C The dates of the First World War are 1914-1918. Complete the questions and answers.

0 A: _When did the war_ start?

   B: It _started_ over seventy years _ago_ .

1 A: _____ did the war continue?

   B: It _____ for five years, _____ 1914 to 1918.

2 A: _____ the war end?

   B: It _____ over seventy years _____ .

3 A: Have many things changed _____ the end of the war?

   B: Yes, many things _____ 1918.

D From the information, write sentences using the words in brackets. Put the verb in the correct tense, and use *for, since,* or *ago.*

0 I haven't seen Bill since his birthday. That was four months ago.

   (I/not/see/Bill/four months) _I haven't seen Bill for four months._

   (I /last/see/Bill/four months/) _I last saw Bill four months ago._

1 We haven't spoken to Jane since her accident. That was two weeks ago.

   (We/not/speak/to Jane/two weeks) _____

   (We/last/speak/to Jane/two weeks/) _____

2 Helen last visited Rome twenty years ago when she was a student.

   (Helen/not/visit/Rome/twenty years) _____

   (Helen/not/visit/Rome/she/be/a student) _____

3 Mary got married two years ago. We haven't seen Mary since her wedding.

   (We/last/see/Mary/two years/) _____

   (We/not/see/Mary/two years) _____

   (We/not/see/her/she/get/married) _____

E Read this text:

> The film 'The Storm' was made in 1972. The stars were Anna Strong and Douglas Wild; they had never met before. The film took eleven months to make, from January to November 1972, and it cost a lot of money. Luckily, it was an enormous success and it was shown in cinemas from 1972 to 1977, and in 1988 and 1990. Anna and Douglas met once in 1992. But they did not see each other again, before Anna died in a car accident in 1993.

Now complete the questions and answers about the text.

0 A: When _was_ 'The Storm' _made_ ?

   B: It _was made_ over 20 years _ago_ .

1 A: _____ Anna and Douglas first meet?

   B: They _____ in 1972, when they made 'The Storm'.

2 A: _____ did the film take to make?

   B: It _____ eleven months to make, _____ January to November.

4 A: When _____ Anna and Douglas _____ meet?

   B: They last _____ in 1992.

5 A: _____ has Anna been dead?

   B: She _____ dead _____ 1993.

42 Defining relative clauses with **who**, **which**, **that** or **whose**

1 If we use a sentence like:
   The police have found the boy.
   it may not be clear which boy. We can make it clear like this:
   *The police have found the boy **who disappeared last week**.*
   Who links the relative clause (**who disappeared last week**) to the main clause (**The police have found the boy**).

2 When we talk about people, we use **that** or **who**:
   *I talked to the girl **that** (or **who**) won the race.*

   When we talk about things or animals, we use **that** or **which**:
   *I like the car **that** (or **which**) won the race.*

3 **That, who,** or **which** can be the subject of the relative clause, like this:

	SUBJECT	
I talked to the girl	**who**	**won.**
	The girl	won.
That is the dog	**that**	**attacked me.**
	The dog	attacked me.

   There is no other pronoun (e.g. **it, they**):
   Not *That is the dog that **it** attacked me.*

4 **That, who,** or **which** can be the object of the relative clause, like this:

	OBJECT	
The card	**which**	*Ken sent* was nice.
Ken sent	the card.	
The man	**that**	*I saw* was very rude.
I saw	the man.	

   There is no other pronoun (e.g. **him, them**):
   Not *The man I saw **him** was very rude.*

   When **that, who,** or **which** is the object of the relative clause (e.g *The card **which** Ken sent*), we can leave them out:
   *The card **Ken sent** was nice.*
   *The man **I saw** was very rude.*

5 Now look at this sentence with **whose**:
   *Susan is the woman **whose husband is an actor**.* (= Susan**'s** husband is an actor.)

   We use **whose** in place of **his, her, their**, etc. We only use it with people, c ountries and organizations, not things. It has a possessive meaning. Here is another example:
   *The man **whose** dog bit me didn't apologise.*
   (= The man didn't apologise. **His** dog bit me.)

....

Practice

A **Complete the sentences using the information in brackets and *who* or *which*.**

0 (I went to see a doctor. She had helped my mother.)
   I went to see the doctor <u>who had helped</u> my mother.

1 (A dog bit me. It belonged to Mrs Jones.)
   The dog _____ belonged to Mrs Jones.

2 (A woman wrote to me. She wanted my advice.)
   The woman _____ wanted my advice.

3 (A bus crashed. It was 23 years old.)
   The bus _____ was 23 years old.

4 (Ann talked to a man. He had won a lot of money.)
   Ann talked to the man _____ .

5 (Mary was staying with her friend. He has a big house in Scotland.)
   Mary was staying with her friend _____ .

6 (He's an architect. He designed the new city library.)
   He's the architect _____ .

B Complete the sentences using the information in brackets and *that*.

0 (Jack made a table. It's not very strong.)

The table _that Jack made_____ is not very strong.

1 (I read about a new computer. I had seen it on TV.)

I read about the new computer _____

2 (Jane made a cake. Nobody liked it.)

Nobody liked the cake _____

3 (Mary sent me a letter. It was very funny.)

The letter _____ was very funny.

4 (My sister wrote an article. The newspaper is going to publish it.)

The newspaper is going to publish the article _____

5 (I met an old lady. She was 103 years old.)

The old lady _____ was 103 years old.

6 (I saw a house. My brother wants to buy it.)

I saw the house _____

C Complete the sentences with one of the phrases in the box and *who* or *whose*.

interviewed me	has visited so many different countries
had saved their son	wives have just had babies
book won a prize last week	divorce was in the papers
car had broken down	complain all the time

0 The parents thanked the woman _who had saved their son._____

0 The couple _whose divorce was in the newspapers_____ have got married again.

1 It is very interesting to meet somebody _____.

2 The person _____ asked me some very difficult questions.

3 In my office there are two men _____.

4 What's the name of that writer _____?

5 I don't like people _____.

6 We helped a woman _____.

D Put in *who* or *that* ONLY IF NECESSARY.

0 The match ___—___ we saw was boring.

0 Did I tell you about the people _who_____ live next door?

0 The horse _that_____ won the race belongs to an Irish woman.

1 I love the ice-cream _____ they sell in that shop.

2 The book _____ I'm reading is about jazz.

3 The woman _____ came to see us was selling magazines.

4 We'll go to a restaurant _____ has a children's menu.

5 The factory _____ closed last week had been there for 70 years.

6 Have you read about the schoolgirl _____ started her own business and is now a millionaire?

7 Jane says that the house _____ Tom has just bought has a beautiful garden.

43 Non-defining relative clauses with **who**, **which** or **whose**

1 Look at these two sentences:

- ▷ *London has over 6 million inhabitants.*
- ▷ *London, **which is the capital of Britain**, has over 6 million inhabitants.*

Which is the capital of Britain gives us more information about London, but we do not need this information to define **London**. We can understand the first sentence without this extra information. **Which is the capital of Britain** is a non-defining relative clause. It has commas (,) to separate it from the rest of the sentence.

2 For things or animals, we use **which** (but not ~~that~~) in non-defining relative clauses:

*Fred sold his computer, **which he no longer needed**, to his cousin. (Not ~~…that he no longer needed…~~)*

*In the summer we stay in my uncle's house, **which is near the sea**.*

3 For people, we use **who** (but not ~~that~~) in non-defining relative clauses. We use **who** when it is the subject of the relative clause:

Elvis Presley, SUBJECT *who died in 1977, earned millions of dollars.*
(**Presley** died in 1977.)

We use **who** (or sometimes **whom**) when it is the object of the relative clause:

My boss, OBJECT *who (or whom) I last saw before Christmas, is very ill.*
(I last saw **my boss** before Christmas.)

4 We use **whose** to mean 'his', 'her', or 'their':

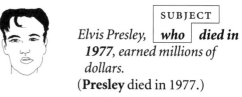

*Marilyn Monroe, **whose real name was Norma Jean**, was born in Los Angeles.*
(**Her** real name was Norma Jean.)

5 We can also use **which** (but not ~~that~~) to refer to a whole fact:

Ann did not want to marry Tom **which** *surprised everybody.*

Here, **which** refers to the fact that Ann did not want to marry Tom.

....

Practice

A **Make one sentence from the two that are given. Use *who* or *which* with the <u>underlined</u> words.**

0 Mont Blanc <u>is between France and Italy</u>. It is the highest mountain in the Alps.

   <u>Mont Blanc, which is between France and Italy, is the highest mountain in the Alps.</u>

0 Alfred Hitchcock <u>was born in Britain</u>. He worked for many years in Hollywood.

   <u>Alfred Hitchcock, who was born in Britain, worked for many years in Hollywood.</u>

1 The sun <u>is really a star</u>. It is 93 million miles from the earth.

   _____

2 John F. Kennedy <u>died in 1963</u>. He was a very famous American President.

   _____

3 Charlie Chaplin <u>was from a poor family</u>. He became a very rich man.

   _____

4 The 1992 Olympics were held in Barcelona. It <u>is in the north-east of Spain</u>.

   _____

5   We went to see the Crown Jewels. They <u>are kept in the Tower of London</u>.

_____

B   **From the notes, make one sentence. Use *who* or *which* with the words in brackets.**

0   Greta Garbo. (She was born in Sweden.) She moved to America in 1925.
    Greta Garbo, who was born in Sweden, moved to America in 1925.

1   Football. (It first started in Britain.) It is now popular in many countries.
    Football, _____

2   Margaret Thatcher. (She was the Prime Minister of Britain for 11 years.) She studied science at university.

    _____

3   Michelangelo. (He lived until he was 90.) He is one of Italy's greatest artists.

    _____

4   The Nile. (It runs through several countries.) It is the longest river in Africa.

    _____

5   Gandhi. (He was born in 1869). He became India's nationalist leader.

    _____

6   Elephants. (They are found in Africa and India). They live to a great age.

    _____

C   **From the notes make one sentence. Use *who* or *which* with the words in brackets.**

0   Martina Navratilova. (She was born in Prague.) She became a US citizen in 1981.
    Martina Navratilova, who was born in Prague, became a US citizen in 1981.

0   Darwin. His ideas changed our view of the world. He travelled to a lot of countries when he was young.
    Darwin, whose ideas changed our view of the world, travelled to a lot of countries when he was
    young.

1   Madonna. (Her parents were born in Italy.) She is a famous American singer.

    _____

2   Bill Clinton. (His wife is a brilliant lawyer.) He became President of the USA in 1993.

    _____

3   Sebastian Coe. (He was a successful English runner.) He is now a politician.

    _____

4   Catherine of Russia. (She ruled for over 30 years.) She made many important changes.

    _____

D   **Underline the words that *which* refers to.**

0   They climbed <u>Snowdon</u>, which is the highest mountain in Wales.

0   <u>They climbed Snowdon</u>, which made them very tired.

1   Maria sang and played the guitar, which everyone enjoyed a lot.

2   The boat stopped at Sousse, which is in Tunisia.

3   The coach stopped at a petrol station, which allowed everyone to get out.

4   We listened to the news, which was in French.

44 Because, in case, so, so that

1 We use **because** to give the reason for something:

	REASON
Jack is in bed	**because** he's got the flu.

We couldn't go out **because** the weather was terrible.
I took a taxi **because** I was in a hurry.

We use **because of** with a noun (e.g. **flu**, **weather**, **noise**):

	REASON
Jack's in bed	**because of** his flu.

We couldn't go out **because of** the storm.
I couldn't sleep **because of** the noise.

2 We use **in case** when the reason is something that might happen:

	REASON
I'm taking an umbrella	**in case** it rains.

(= I'm taking an umbrella **because** it **might** rain.)

I'll phone John now, **in case** he wants to come with us. (= ... **because** he **might** want to come with us.)

3 We use **so** to talk about the result of something:

	RESULT
I was in a hurry	**so** I took a taxi.

Jack has got the flu **so** he's in bed.
The weather was terrible **so** we couldn't go out.
My neighbours were having a party and making a lot of noise **so** I couldn't sleep.

4 We use **so that** to talk about the purpose of an action:

	PURPOSE
I took a taxi	**so that** I would arrive on time.

I listen to the news in the morning **so that** I know what's happening in the world.
Tom goes jogging every day **so that** he won't get fat.
I took a taxi **so that** my friends would not have to wait for me.
(We can also use **to** + infinitive to talk about purpose; see unit 29.)

Practice

A Write each sentence in a different way using the words given.

0 Tom didn't want to go out because he had a cold.

<u>Tom didn't want to go out</u> because of <u>his cold.</u>

0 Take some money because you might need to take a taxi.

<u>Take some money</u> in case <u>you need to take a taxi.</u>

0 John and I asked for a drink because we were thirsty.

<u>John and I were thirsty</u> so <u>we asked for a drink.</u>

1 Mary went to bed because she was tired.

_____ so _____

2 I couldn't sleep because it was so hot.

_____ the heat.

3 Jill doesn't like apples so she doesn't eat them.

_____ because _____

4 The streets were crowded because of the football match.

_____ there was a football match.

5 I'll give Jane a key to the house because she might get home before me.
_____ in case _____

B Complete the sentences with *because, in case,* or *so,* and a phrase from the box. Use each phrase once.

I'll take a book to read	I want to lose weight
she's at home	~~they had to wait for the next one~~
his passport was out of date	his wife was ill
there is a power cut this weekend	

0 They missed one bus _so they had to wait for the next one._

1 I don't know where my sister is, but I'll try phoning her _____

2 I'm eating less these days _____

3 Peter had trouble at the airport _____

4 It's a long journey _____

5 We've bought some candles _____

6 Mr Smith didn't go to the meeting _____

C Complete each sentence using *so that* and one of the phrases in the box.

she can be nearer her work
~~I know what's in the news~~
they can keep in contact with each other
everybody would know our new address
they can keep their clothes clean

0 I read the newspaper every day _so that I know what's in the news._

1 We sent cards to all our friends _____

2 Scientists and doctors wear white coats _____

3 Policemen carry radios _____

4 Mary is moving to Bristol _____

D Write out complete sentences from the words in brackets, making any necessary changes and including *so that.*

0 (Mark/go/swimming every day /he can stay healthy)
   Mark goes swimming every day so that he can stay healthy.

1 (Last week, my brother/lend/me £20/I could buy some new shoes)
   _____

2 (Last month, the Government/pass/new traffic laws/fewer people will have accidents)
   _____

3 (Our school has/open/a new library /we can have more books)
   _____

4 (Ann always/write/everything in her diary/she doesn't forget her appointments)
   _____

5 (Last Friday, we/leave/home early/we could avoid the morning traffic)
   _____

Grammar and spelling tables

Table A   Plural nouns

	SINGULAR	PLURAL
With most nouns we add -s to make them plural:	shop tyre kilo	shops tyres kilos
With nouns that end with -s, -ss, -sh, -ch, -x, we add -es:	bus dress wish beach box	buses dresses wishes beaches boxes
With some nouns that end with -o, we add -es:	tomato potato	tomatoes potatoes
We change -f/-fe to -ves in the plural:	thief shelf leaf life	thieves shelves leaves lives
With nouns that end with a consonant* + -y, we change the -y to -ies:	story copy lorry	stories copies lorries
Irregular nouns	tooth child woman	teeth children women

Table B   Uncountable nouns

These are some common uncountable nouns:	ice, water, rain, snow, heat, noise cotton, glass, petrol, money, luggage information, work, homework, advice, news meat, milk, butter, bread, marmalade, food, tea, coffee, sugar, toast, cheese
Uncountable nouns do not have a plural form:	petrol (Not petrols) bread (Not breads)
We cannot use a/an with an uncountable noun, but we can use some/any, the, much (not many), such, and my/your/his etc:	a: *I always have an egg, and then* **toast** *and* **marmalade** *for breakfast.* some: *I'd like* **some tea** *please.* the: *Look at* **the snow** *outside.* much: *How* **much luggage** *have you got?* such: *We've had* **such wonderful news**.
Some nouns can be countable or uncountable:	*I heard* **a noise** *from downstairs.* (countable) *I can't sleep. The neighbours are making* **so much noise**. (uncountable)

Table C Present Simple

	I/you/we/they	He/she/it
After **he/she/it**, we add **-s** to most Present Simple verbs:	say make advise	says makes advises
We add **-es** to verbs that end with **-ss**, **-sh**, **-ch**, **-o** (e.g. *finish*, *go*):	pass finish wish catch go do	passes finishes wishes catches goes does
We change **-y** to **-ies** with verbs that end with a consonant* + **-y**:	fly carry study	flies carries studies

Table D **-ing** forms

	INFINITIVE	**-ing** FORM
With most verbs we add **-ing**:	go ask	going asking
With verbs that end with a consonant* + **-e**, we delete the **-e** and add **-ing**:	take hope live queue	taking hoping living queuing
With verbs that end with **-ie**, we change **-ie** to **-ying**:	lie die	lying dying
With verbs that end with one vowel* + one consonant (e.g. *run*, *swim*, *jog*), we double the consonant:	get run swim jog	getting running swimming jogging
But note that we do not double the consonant, (1) when it is a **y** or **w** (e.g. *stay*), (2) when the last syllable* is not stressed (e.g. *VISit*, *LISten*, *WONder*):	stay buy borrow draw visit listen wonder	staying buying borrowing drawing visiting listening wondering
But note also that we double the **l** at the end of verbs, when the last syllable is not stressed (e.g. *TRAvel*):	travel	travelling

---

* Consonants: b c d f g h j k l m n p q r s t v w x y z
Vowels: a e i o u
Syllables: | *hit* |=1 syllable | *vi* | *sit* |=2 syllables | *re* | *mem* | *ber* |=3 syllables

Table E Regular verbs: Past Simple and past participle

	INFINITIVE	PAST SIMPLE	PAST PARTICIPLE
With most verbs we add **-ed**:	**happen**	**happened**	**happened**
With verbs ending with **-e**, we add **-d**:	**live**	**lived**	**lived**
With verbs that end with a consonant* + **-y**, we change the **y** to **-ied**:	**try** **study**	**tried** **studied**	**tried** **studied**
With verbs that end with one vowel* + one consonant , we double the consonant:	**stop** **grab**	**stopped** **grabbed**	**stopped** **grabbed**
We do not double the consonant, (1) when it is a **y** or **w** (e.g. *enjoy*), (2) when the last syllable* is not stressed (e.g. *disCOVer, LISten, HAppen*):	**enjoy** **allow** **discover** **listen**	**enjoyed** **allowed** **discovered** **listened**	**enjoyed** **allowed** **discovered** **listened**
But note also that we double the **l** at the end of verbs, when the last syllable is not stressed (e.g. *TRAvel*):	**cancel** **travel**	**cancelled** **travelled**	**cancelled** **travelled**

Table F Irregular verbs: Past Simple and past participle

INFINITIVE	PAST SIMPLE	PAST PARTICIPLE	INFINITIVE	PAST SIMPLE	PAST PARTICIPLE
be	was/were	been	give	gave	given
beat	beat	beaten	go	went	gone/been
become	became	become	grow	grew	grown
begin	began	begun	have	had	had
break	broke	broken	hear	heard	heard
bring	brought	brought	hide	hid	hidden
build	built	built	hit	hit	hit
burn	burnt	burnt	hold	held	held
buy	bought	bought	hurt	hurt	hurt
catch	caught	caught	keep	kept	kept
choose	chose	chosen	know	knew	known
come	came	come	learn	learnt/learned	learnt/learned
cost	cost	cost	leave	left	left
cut	cut	cut	lend	lent	lent
do	did	done	let	let	let
draw	drew	drawn	lose	lost	lost
drink	drank	drunk	make	made	made
drive	drove	driven	meet	met	met
eat	ate	eaten	pay	paid	paid
fall	fell	fallen	put	put	put
feel	felt	felt	read	read	read
find	found	found	ring	rang	rung
fly	flew	flown	run	ran	run
forget	forgot	forgotten	say	said	said
forbid	forbade	forbidden	see	saw	seen
get	got	got	sell	sold	sold

INFINITIVE	PAST SIMPLE	PAST PARTICIPLE		INFINITIVE	PAST SIMPLE	PAST PARTICIPLE
send	sent	sent		swim	swam	swum
show	showed	shown/showed		take	took	taken
shut	shut	shut		teach	taught	taught
sing	sang	sung		tell	told	told
sit	sat	sat		think	thought	thought
sleep	slept	slept		throw	threw	thrown
speak	spoke	spoken		understand	understood	understood
spend	spent	spent		wake	woke	woken
stand	stood	stood		wear	wore	worn
steal	stole	stolen		win	won	won
sweep	swept	swept		write	wrote	written

Table G   Comparative and superlative adjectives

	ADJECTIVE	COMPARATIVE	SUPERLATIVE
We add **-er /-est** to short adjectives (one-syllable* adjectives):	cheap near long	cheaper nearer longer	the cheapest the nearest the longest
We add **-r/-st** to adjectives that end with **-e**:	late	later	the latest
With short adjectives that end with one vowel* and one consonant* (e.g. *big*), we double the consonant:	big hot wet	bigger hotter wetter	the biggest the hottest the wettest
We don't double **w**:	few	fewer	the fewest
We use **more / the most** before adjectives of two or more syllables*:	expensive beautiful polluted	more expensive more beautiful more polluted	the most expensive the most beautiful the most polluted
But note that with adjectives ending with **-y** (e.g. *happy*), we change **-y** to **-ier /-iest**:	happy lucky easy dirty	happier luckier easier dirtier	the happiest the luckiest the easiest the dirtiest
Irregular adjectives:	good bad far little	better worse farther less	the best the worst the farthest the least
fewer and **less** Note that we usually use **fewer** with plural nouns, and **less** with uncountable nouns (e.g. **money**):	*There are **fewer shops** in the centre of town than there used to be.* *John earns **less money** than Mary.*		

* Consonants: b c d f g h j k l m n p q r s t v w x y z
Vowels: a e i o u
Syllables: |*hit*|=1 syllable |*vi*|*sit*|=2 syllables |*re*|*mem*|*ber*|=3 syllables

Exit tests

You can do these tests when you have finished studying the units in this book, to see if there are units that you should look at again. In the tests, each question relates to the unit with the same number, e.g. question 1 tests something from unit 1, question 2 tests something from unit 2, etc.

Exit test 1

Choose the right answer (**a**, **b**, **c**) and write **a**, **b**, or **c** in the box, as in the example. The correct answers are on page 117.

0 John always **a** get up **b** gets up **c** is getting up every morning at six o'clock. | b |

1 The Queen **a** don't live **b** doesn't live **c** don't lives in Edinburgh. | |

2 In the photo, a dog **a** are running **b** is running **c** running after a cat. | |

3 Look! Two policemen **a** come **b** is coming **c** are coming this way. | |

4 That sign **a** is meaning **b** mean **c** means that we must be quiet. | |

5 When **a** did you leave **b** you left **c** you did leave school? | |

6 When the phone rang, I couldn't answer it because I **a** had **b** have had **c** was having a bath. | |

7 When we were young, we **a** swim **b** were swimming **c** used to swim every day. | |

8 I **a** did never eat **b** has never eaten **c** have never eaten horse meat. | |

9 What date **a** have you sent **b** did you send **c** you have sent that letter? | |

10 Mrs Buxton **a** taught **b** has taught **c** is teaching at that school since 1993. | |

11 We have **a** invited **b** been inviting **c** being invited 200 people to our party. | |

12 When I got home there was nobody there. Everybody **a** was going **b** went **c** had gone to the cinema. | |

13 Pam has asked me to play tennis with her. We **a** will **b** are going **c** will go to play on Saturday. | |

14 If Elvis Presley was alive today, he **a** will **b** would **c** should be over 60 years old. | |

15 If Tom had studied hard, he **a** had **b** would **c** would have passed his exams. | |

16 If Jane's team wins next Saturday, she **a** will be **b** is **c** would be very happy. | |

17 When did your sister **a** make **b** do **c** get married? | |

18 You can **a** look after **b** get up **c** look up the new words in your dictionary. | |

19 When Peter was a boy, he **a** wasn't able **b** couldn't **c** wouldn't swim very well. | |

20 I can see Mary's car in the car park, so she **a** can't **b** can **c** must be here somewhere. | |

21 In towns you have to drive slowly. You **a** don't have to   **b** mustn't   **c** haven't to drive faster than 50 kph.

22 My brother **a** doesn't need   **b** don't need   **c** needn't new football boots.

23 If you find someone's passport, you **a** had better   **b** ought   **c** should to give it to the police.

24 Susan usually works from Monday to Friday, but last week she **a** should have   **b** must   **c** had to work on Saturday as well.

25 In the old days, bottles **a** are made   **b** were made   **c** were making by hand.

26 We can't use the car because it **a** is mended.   **b** hasn't mended.   **c** is being mended.

27 Tomorrow I'm going to **a** have cut my hair   **b** cut my hair   **c** have my hair cut at the new hairdresser's.

28 All my family enjoy **a** to go   **b** go   **c** going for long walks.

29 Jane has gone to the shop **a** to   **b** for   **c** for buying some eggs.

30 Ann wanted **a** that I have   **b** me to   **c** that I should have lunch with her.

31 **a** How is she?   **b** What is she like?   **c** What does she like? ~ She's very nice.

32 I hear you went to Scotland last summer. **a** How many times   **b** How far   **c** How long did you stay there?

33 Peter **a** told me   **b** said me   **c** told that he was going to be away this week.

34 I asked **a** he   **b** them   **c** she to help me.

35 He asked **a** I   **b** her   **c** she if she was Japanese.

36 My mother **a** is   **b** is an   **c** is a university teacher.

37 If you're hungry, **a** there's   **b** it's   **c** they are some food in the fridge.

38 I've never seen **a** such   **b** so much   **c** so enormous apples.

39 I like classical music. I'm **a** fond of   **b** pleased with   **c** like Beethoven, for example.

40 The birds were sitting **a** at   **b** in   **c** on the telephone wires.

41 This house was built **a** for 600 years.   **b** since 600 years.   **c** 600 years ago.

42 Was Mary the woman **a** who   **b** that she   **c** which came to see you last week?

43 Edinburgh, **a** which   **b** who   **c** that is the capital of Scotland, is well worth a visit.

44 We couldn't hear the speaker **a** because of   **b** because   **c** in case the noise from the street.

Total:

44

Exit test 2

Choose the right answer (**a**, **b**, **c**) and write **a**, **b**, or **c** in the box, as in the example. .

0   Ann **a** don't like   **b** like   **c** doesn't like her new house.   `c`

1   Cars **a** doesn't use   **b** don't use   **c** not uses coal.

2   Jill isn't at home. She **a** staying   **b** are staying   **c** is staying with her cousin this week.

3   A police car sometimes **a** is stopping   **b** stop   **c** stops in front of our house.

4   We **a** aren't knowing   **b** aren't know   **c** don't know their names.

5   My sisters **a** didn't like   **b** not like   **c** liked the concert. They hated it.

6   I saw the accident. I **a** was waiting   **b** waited   **c** am waiting for the bus when it happened.

7   I **a** was smoking   **b** used to smoking   **c** used to smoke years ago, but I don't now.

8   Our address is 23, Brook Road. We **a** lived   **b** are living   **c** have lived there for almost 10 years.

9   Tom **a** just has   **b** just   **c** has just gone to the shops.

10 Half an hour ago someone **a** has come   **b** came   **c** come to see you.

11 All the runners are very tired. They have **a** been run   **b** run   **c** been running for two hours.

12 It was raining when I woke up this morning, but when I left home to go to work the rain **a** has   **b** is   **c** had stopped.

13 In the year 2006, it **a** will be   **b** is being   **c** going to be 250 years since Mozart was born.

14 I live in London, but I wish I **a** would live   **b** lived   **c** have lived in a small town.

15 I wish I **a** would have gone   **b** have been gone   **c** had gone to Jean's party last night.

16 If Tom really loved Jane, he **a** will   **b** did   **c** would ask her to marry him.

17 Parents often say to their children that they must **a** make   **b** do   **c** get their homework before they watch TV.

18 If your clothes are wet, take **a** off.   **b** off them.   **c** them off.

19 I've got a problem. **a** May   **b** Shall   **c** Could you help me, please?

20 I'm not sure where Anne is, but she **a** may be   **b** is   **c** must be in her room.

21 Tell Mark that he **a** doesn't have   **b** mustn't   **c** hasn't to come tomorrow if he's got other things to do.

22 There was plenty of food, so we **a** needn't **b** needn't have **c** need bought any more. ☐

23 Jane isn't very well. We **a** should **b** ought **c** had better to go and visit her. ☐

24 Sara **a** must go **b** had to go **c** should have gone to Edinburgh last Saturday, but she was ill and so she stayed in bed. ☐

25 The window **a** was smashing **b** smashed **c** was smashed by a ball. ☐

26 We couldn't meet at our house, because it **a** was being **b** was **c** has been painted. ☐

27 My mother **a** had taken her photo **b** had her photo taken **c** her photo was taken by a well-known photographer. ☐

28 I don't want to see a film. I'd like **a** going **b** to go **c** that we go to a restaurant. ☐

29 I borrowed Anna's van **a** to transport **b** for transport **c** for transporting the furniture I had bought. ☐

30 Jane let me **a** borrow **b** borrowing **c** to borrow her car. ☐

31 In the film Julie seems a very serious person. **a** What she likes **b** What's she like **c** What does she like in real life? ☐

32 **a** How far is it **b** How long is it **c** How long is there from here to Newcastle? ☐

33 What did Carol say? ~ She **a** said me **b** told **c** said she would help us, but she hasn't come. ☐

34 She told **a** to them **b** them to **c** them be quiet. ☐

35 I asked **a** if them **b** whether they **c** whether them were ready. ☐

36 Are you thirsty? Would you like **a** glass **b** the glass **c** a glass of water? ☐

37 When I was young, **a** there were **b** it was **c** they were 12 cinemas in this town. ☐

38 I'm pleased Jane's here. She's **a** such a **b** such **c** so nice person. ☐

39 Bob is very fond **a** of visiting **b** to visit **c** about visiting old churches. ☐

40 My birthday is **a** in **b** on **c** at March. ☐

41 We have lived in this house **a** for **b** during **c** since 30 years. ☐

42 The car **a** I saw **b** I saw it **c** that I saw it was going very fast. ☐

43 The Eiffel Tower, **a** that **b** who **c** which was built in 1889, is still very popular with tourists. ☐

44 Peter arrived at the airport early **a** because **b** so that **c** in case he would not miss his plane. ☐

Total: ☐

44

Answer key to practice exercises

Unit 1

A 1 cycles … goes
2 says … does … catches
3 buys … does
4 likes … gets
5 lives … works
6 leave … finishes
7 rides … carries
8 eats … has

B 1 Do modern trains use coal? ~ No, they don't. They use electricity.
2 Does the Queen often wear a crown? ~ No, she doesn't. She usually wears a hat.
3 Does wine come from oranges? ~ No, it doesn't. It comes from grapes.
4 Does Sri Lanka export coffee? ~ No, it doesn't. It exports tea.
5 Do potatoes grow on bushes? ~ No, they don't. They grow in the ground.

C 1 Modern trains don't use coal.
2 The Queen doesn't often wear a crown.
3 Wine doesn't come from oranges.
4 Sri Lanka doesn't export coffee.
5 Potatoes don't grow on bushes.

D 1 Ice floats on water.
2 Lions don't live in the Arctic.
3 Winter doesn't come after spring.
4 Austrians speak German.
5 Cotton doesn't come from sheep.

E 1 Neil cycles every day. He never drinks beer.
2 Mary swims every weekend. She smokes 15 cigarettes a day.
3 Bill plays tennis once a week. He doesn't smoke.
4 Susan swims twice a week. She doesn't drink alcohol.

Unit 2

A 1 It is/It's running
2 She is/She's painting
3 He is/He's washing
4 They are/They're eating
5 They are/They're looking

B 1 is/'s doing a computer course this week.

2 am/'m going to work by bus this week.
3 are/'re sleeping in the sitting-room at the moment.

C 1 Fashions are changing all the time these days.
2 More women are studying at university these days.
3 House prices are going up all the time nowadays.
4 The sea is getting dirtier every year.

D 1 Because she is always asking me for money.
2 Because they are always arguing.
3 Because she is always borrowing my CDs.
4 Because he is always phoning me late at night.

Unit 3

A 1 lives … works
2 is staying … is/'s working
3 is staying … is/'s working
4 lives … works
5 lives … works
6 is staying … is working

B 1 No, they are getting things ready for the next competition.
How often do they have these competitions?
2 Why is that machine not working at the moment?
I don't know, but a mechanic is mending it.
What does the machine do in fact? Does it make boxes?
Yes, it makes boxes of all sizes.
3 Look! The Fosters are working in their garden.
They don't usually work on Sundays.
Are you getting ready for the winter?
Yes, we're tidying up the leaves.
We always try to do it before the winter comes.
4 Sam, what are you looking for?
I'm looking for Jean's glasses.
She doesn't often wear them.
She only wears them to read, so she often loses them.

Unit 4

A 1 is sitting
     2 is listening
     3 is playing
     4 think
     5 like
     6 understand
     7 Do … want
     8 drink

B 1 are listening … is looking
     2 are counting … do not/don't know
     3 likes … fit
     4 is sitting … does not/doesn't matter
     5 costs … includes

C 1 Do you recognize the woman in this photo? … Do you mean the woman who is looking straight at the camera?
     2 Hello, David. Why are you standing here? Are you waiting for me? … Yes, I want to speak to you.
     3 Listen to the engine. Do you think it is all right? … It sounds all right, but it smells of oil.

D 1 is thinking
     2 has
     3 is tasting
     4 feels
     5 tastes
     6 is having
     7 thinks

Unit 5

A 1 What did Marie Curie discover in 1898? ~ She discovered radium.
     2 Where did Michelangelo live? ~ He lived in Florence.
     3 When did Margaret Thatcher become Prime Minister? ~ She became Prime Minister in 1979.
     4 What did Alexander Bell invent? ~ He invented the telephone.
     5 How many books did Agatha Christie write? ~ She wrote over a hundred books.
     6 When did Greta Garbo move to the United States? ~ She moved there in 1925.

B 1 When Bob's sister was at university, she wrote a lot of poetry.
     2 When Fred was in the army, he went to many different countries.

     3 When Jane and Michael were at school, they didn't do much homework.
     4 When Anna was a teenager, she wore very long skirts.

C 1 I made friends with a man called Harry.
     2 Sometimes we talked about our ideas for a holiday.
     3 We decided to go together to Rome.
     4 We went by train, of course.
     5 The journey lasted over 24 hours.
     6 Of course, we saw all the famous buildings in Rome. They were fascinating.
     7 But most of all, we enjoyed the delicious Italian food.
     8 In particular, we ate some mushrooms that were as big as a plate.
     9 We told everyone about the size of the mushrooms when we got back home.
    10 But nobody believed us.

Unit 6

A 1 The storm started while they were driving home .
     2 I saw an accident while I was waiting for the bus.
     3 Mary went to several concerts while she was staying in London.
     4 My father was cooking the dinner when he burnt his fingers.
     5 The soldiers were preparing to leave when the bomb exploded.

B 1 made … was making … arrived … helped
     2 designed … started … was working … died
     3 escaped … were taking … caught … locked
     4 were losing … won
     5 sang … played … recorded … was preparing … shot
     6 were coming … were hurrying … was standing … grabbed

C 1 did you do
     2 you were reading
     3 rang
     4 were you doing
     5 was drinking
     6 drank
     7 went
     8 did you put
     9 was raining

Unit 7

A 1 Last Sunday Mike stayed at home, but he normally goes fishing.
2 We usually swim in the sea, but last Sunday we swam in the river.
3 Last summer, Bob had a short holiday, but he usually has a long holiday.
4 Mrs Jones normally sleeps for seven hours every night, but last night she slept for nine hours.
5 I usually enjoy the food in this restaurant, but I did not/didn't like it yesterday.
6 Peter usually does his homework, but he didn't do it yesterday.

B 1 Does … have
2 Did … wake up
3 Did … send
4 Does … phone

C 1 used to eat … he eats
2 used to drink … she drinks
3 eats … she used to eat
4 eats … she used to eat
5 Did Robert use to eat …
6 Did Mary use to eat …
7 Did Pam use to drink …
8 didn't use to eat
9 didn't use to eat
10 didn't use to drink

Unit 8

A 1 Has Tom bought anything? ~ Yes, he has/he's bought a new suit.
2 Has Jane given him any money? ~ Yes, she has/she's given him £10.
3 Have you broken anything? ~ Yes, I have/I've broken a plate.
4 Has Pam chosen a present? ~ Yes, she has/she's chosen this novel.
5 Have they brought any food? ~ Yes, they have/they've brought some sandwiches.

B 1 Somebody has opened the garage door.
2 Somebody has eaten all the biscuits.
3 Somebody has broken the kitchen window.
4 Somebody has stolen Mary's watch.
5 Somebody has drunk my orange juice.
6 Somebody has taken my shoes.

C 1 He has/He's already made copies of the letter.
2 He has not/hasn't put the copies in the envelopes yet.
3 He has/He's already written the text of the advertisement.
4 He has not/hasn't sent the advertisement to the paper yet.

D 1 Has Sue won any tennis competitions this year? ~ Yes, she has/she's won three this year.
2 Have you shaved today? ~ No, I have not/haven't shaved since yesterday.
3 Have you sold many TVs this month? ~ Yes, we have/we've sold 23 this month.
4 Have you played tennis this week? ~ No, I have not/haven't played for a month.

Unit 9

A 1 won
2 painted
3 went
4 died
5 married

B 1 I met Brian
2 I was in the garden
3 she loved swimming.
4 I bought these shoes
5 he had very long hair.
6 he smiled.

C 1 Don't know.
2 Yes.
3 Yes.
4 Don't know.

D 1 B: Jane has had a baby boy
    A: When did she have the baby?
2 B: Mary has broken my camera.
    A: How did she break it?
3 B: My bicycle has disappeared.
    A: Where did you leave it?
4 B: He has lost his bag.
    A: When did he lose it?
5 B: I have/I've passed my exam.
    A: What mark did you get?

E 1 Kathy has just come home.
2 Colin finished his lunch a few minutes ago.
3 Michael had a shower a few minutes ago.
4 Jenny has just gone to bed.

Unit 10

A
1 won … have won
2 has made … did … make
3 was … has been
4 did … work … has worked
5 have earned … earned
6 did … rain … has … rained

B
1 studied … wrote
2 has developed … has made
3 worked … spent
4 has won … has earned

C
1 Anna and John have lived in London since their wedding.
2 Mary has worked in France for 6 months.
3 Pam hasn't played tennis since she was 15.
4 Fred stopped eating meat 2 years ago.

D
1 did you finish
2 came
3 have you lived
4 moved
5 have been
6 left
7 Have you seen
8 phoned
9 met
10 have not seen

Unit 11

A
1 We have sold much more than we expected.
2 How much money have you spent this week?
3 How many people has Jane invited to her party?
4 It has been raining for hours.
5 They have been drilling holes in the wall all morning.
6 How long have you been sitting here?

B
1 have been doing the washing-up.
2 has peeled
3 have been cutting the grass.
4 have been defrosting the fridge.
5 has swept
6 have been peeling the onions.
7 has done the washing-up.
8 has defrosted it.

C
1 been standing … been queuing
2 had … broken
3 left … been sitting … noticed

Unit 12

A
1 had never ridden a horse
2 had already run in five marathons
3 had never written a poem
4 had never appeared on TV
5 had already played tennis at Wimbledon four times
6 had already written two novels

B
1 When the firemen arrived, we had already put the fire out.
2 When the manager came back, Jim had already finished the work.
3 When Philip telephoned, I had already gone to bed.
4 When their children came home, Alice and Jack had already had lunch.
5 When his wife got home from work, Ian had already prepared the supper.
6 The thieves had already spent the money, when the police caught them.

C
1 had just gone out.
2 had been to Cambridge.
3 had made some sandwiches.
4 had met her in Amsterdam.
5 had ever been to Japan.

Unit 13

A
1 will beat
2 will lose to
3 will draw with
4 will beat
5 will lose to

B
1 'm going to see her
2 'll go to the hairdresser's
3 's going to have a shower
4 'll take it to the car wash

C
1 I will/I'll buy the tickets before I go to work.
2 As soon as Henry arrives, we will/we'll have something to eat.
3 The play will start after the music stops.
4 He will not/won't stop until he finishes the job.
5 When John gets here, we will/we'll go to the beach.

D
1 is/'s having supper with Jill and Kate.
2 is going to tidy her room.
3 is/'s going to wash her hair.
4 is/'s meeting Tim at the airport.

Unit 14

A 1 she would go
2 she lived
3 he didn't eat
4 he would have
5 she got
6 he wouldn't smoke

B 1 they discovered oil in Ireland
2 doctors found a cure for cancer
3 young people stopped buying pop records
4 astronauts visited Mars

C 1 I had good eyesight.
2 I could speak German.
3 I had a degree.
4 I was/were 18.

D 1 were fewer cars
2 drove more slowly
3 would have more time for reading
4 ate fewer sweets
5 more people travelled by bus
6 had more time to cook … would eat less 'fast food'

Unit 15

A 1 If she had spoken German very well, she would have applied for the job.
2 If her friend hadn't phoned, she wouldn't have heard about the teaching jobs.
3 If she hadn't contacted the company, they wouldn't have asked her to go for an interview.
4 If the interview had gone badly, the director wouldn't have offered Ellen a job.
5 If Ellen had known some Spanish, she would have started at once.
6 If she hadn't been good at languages, she wouldn't have made rapid progress.

B 1 had not lost … would have phoned
2 had not broken … would have gone
3 would have made … had not forgotten

C 1 I had told the truth.
2 wishes he hadn't borrowed some money from his mother.
3 wishes she had got up early.
4 wishes he had gone to the party.
5 wish I had sent Jill a birthday card.
6 Fiona wishes she had helped her sister.
7 He wishes he hadn't shouted at the children.

Unit 16

A 1 if you heat gold to 1063 degrees, it melts.
2 if you heat alcohol to 78 degrees, it boils.
3 if you heat silver to 960 degrees, it melts.

B 1 comes … will/'ll go
2 writes … will/'ll tell
3 will forgive … pays
4 will feel … stops
5 needs … will/'ll lend
6 listens … will/'ll know

C 1 might
2 will
3 will
4 might … might

D 1 unless you telephone first.
2 if they don't invite you.
3 if you can't swim.
4 unless we win on Saturday.

E 1 wouldn't be able to move about so easily in the dark.
2 wouldn't be able to recognize people
3 wouldn't be able to help blind people.
4 wouldn't be able to remember everything
5 Horses wouldn't be able to pull heavy loads

Unit 17

A 1 arrive
2 became
3 buy
4 received
5 buy
6 receive
7 becomes
8 arrived

B 1 got engaged … got married … got divorced
2 get undressed
3 got stuck
4 get lost
5 get washed
6 get drunk
7 get confused

C 1 does
2 does
3 makes
4 makes
5 make
6 do
7 do
8 do

D 1 make a difficult decision
2 made any friends
3 made a mistake
4 do all the boring work
5 make much difference
6 do a boring job
7 do your best
8 making an effort

Unit 18

A 1 coming round
2 look after
3 calling for
4 go out
5 put on
6 get off
7 join in
8 get back

B 1 fill in
2 Hold on!
3 get at
4 went off
5 rubbed out
6 look up
7 brought back
8 put away

C 1 looked for them
2 turn them off
3 handed it in
4 agree with him
5 drew it out
6 let it out

Unit 19

A 1 could type 15 words per minute … he can type 30 words per minute
2 can lift 100 kilos … he'll be able to join a weightlifting team
3 could speak a little French … she can speak French quite well
4 can cook quite well … she'll be able to work as a chef
5 could only play the piano … he can play the piano and the violin … he'll be able to be a professional musician
6 could ride a bike … she can drive a car … she'll be able to drive a racing car

B 1 could
2 Could … Shall
3 can … Can't … MAY

4 Shall … can't … 'll … 'll be able to … managed to
5 Could … can … can't … I'll

Unit 20

A 1 must like
2 can't come
3 can't belong
4 can't live
5 must have
6 must remember
7 can't want
8 must spend

B 1 can't be … could be
2 can't be … could be
3 can't be … could be
4 can't be … could be
5 could be … can't be
6 must be Smith.

C 1 might go to Portugal
2 must cost a lot of money
3 might come this weekend
4 can't take much interest
5 must work long hours
6 might be at the gym … might also be at the shops

Unit 21

A 1 They don't have to go now.
2 Mark mustn't speak to my cousin.
3 You don't have to drive slowly here.
4 Alice doesn't have to get up early.
5 The children mustn't play in the park.
6 Mike doesn't have to phone his brother.

B 1 Does Jim have to go to the doctor's? ~ Yes, he does.
2 Do we have to show our passports? ~ Yes, we do.
3 Does Linda have to pay? ~ No, she doesn't.
4 Do they have to do all this work today? ~ Yes, they do.

C 1 mustn't park
2 must obey
3 mustn't play
4 must be
5 mustn't work

D 1 must … don't have to
2 don't have to … mustn't

3 mustn't … don't have to
4 must … must

E 1 has
2 Does she
3 have to
4 she has
5 must
6 does she
7 mustn't

Unit 22

A 1 Does Fred need a ladder? ~ Yes, he does.
2 Do we need to go to the shops? ~ No, we don't.
3 Does John need to leave before lunch? ~ No, he doesn't.
4 Do they need to check the train times? ~ Yes,they do.

B 1 We don't need a lot of paper.
2 Mark needn't get everything ready today.
3 Mary needn't leave at six o'clock.
4 Ann doesn't need a new bag.

C 1 For maths exams, students need to bring pens and pencils.
2 For football competitions, students needn't bring shirts.
3 For drawing exams, students needn't bring paper.
4 For art exams, students need to bring brushes.
5 For tennis competitions, students needn't bring balls.
6 For football competitions, students need to bring shorts and boots.
7 For maths exams, students needn't bring rubbers.
8 For drawing exams, students need to bring rulers and pencils.

D 1 needn't have gone
2 needn't phone
3 needn't have bought
4 needn't have worked
5 needn't pay

Unit 23

A 1 try
2 start
3 listen
4 have
5 to wait

B 1 You ought not to move it.
2 They had better not come after supper.
3 We should not change everything.
4 You'd better not tell the director.

C 1 shouldn't move the person yourself … should call an ambulance
2 should give you a new cup
3 shouldn't let him eat so much … should make him do lots of sport
4 shouldn't touch anything … should leave everything where it is
5 shouldn't drive home in her car … should ask someone to take her
6 shouldn't borrow money

D 1 they had/they'd better clear everything away
2 we had/we'd better take our umbrellas
3 I had/I'd better go to bed early too

Unit 24

A 1 did not/didn't have to … had to
2 did you have to … had to
3 Did you have to … had to
4 did you have to … had to … did not/didn't have to
5 Did they have to … did not/didn't have to … had to

B 1 should have bought
2 shouldn't have gone
3 shouldn't have eaten
4 should have locked
5 shouldn't have borrowed

B 1 Colin had to work on Sunday.
2 Joan didn't have to work on Sunday.
3 Derek should have worked on Sunday
4 Mary didn't have to work on Saturday.
5 Brian should have worked on Saturday
6 Daniel had to work on Saturday.
7 Joan should have worked on Saturday
8 Derek didn't have to work on Saturday.

Unit 25

A 1 The planet Pluto was discovered in 1930.
2 Two atomic bombs were dropped on Japan in 1945.
3 John F. Kennedy was killed in Dallas.
4 The first Apple computers were produced in the 1970s.
5 The Eiffel Tower was built a hundred years ago.

6 The first jet planes were made in Germany.
7 The Taj Mahal was built in the 17th century.
8 In 1957, millions of pounds were stolen from a train.
9 Queen Elizabeth was crowned in 1953.
10 In the old days, horses were used for transport.
11 The first books were printed in the 15th century.
12 Everest was climbed for the first time in 1953.

B 1 The drug penicillin was dicovered by Alexander Fleming.
2 The song 'Yesterday' was written by the Beatles.
3 The detective Hercule Poirot was created by Agatha Christie.
4 The 'Eroica' symphony was composed by Beethoven.
5 'Gone with the Wind' was written by Margaret Mitchell.
6 The telephone was invented by Alexander Bell.
7 The jet engine was designed by Frank Whittle.
8 'Jurassic Park' was directed by Steven Spielberg.
9 The 'Mona Lisa' was painted by Leonardo da Vinci.

C 1 was given some flowers.
2 was offered a wonderful job.
3 will be given a present.
4 was sent a strange letter.
5 will be paid over five hundred pounds.
6 has been promised a bicycle for her birthday.
7 was given the Nobel Prize for Chemistry in 1911.
8 We weren't told the truth.

Unit 26

A 1 are made
2 was being built
3 must be typed
4 have been cleaned
5 were broken
6 has been stolen

B 1 was Mary examined?
2 will the food be prepared?
3 has this window been broken?

C 1 was not examined this morning.
2 will not be prepared on Friday.
3 has not been broken three times.

D 1 has been won by the French team.
2 were being trained by a woman.
3 can be played by people of all ages.
4 was being watched by a large crowd.
5 was sent by the secretary.
6 have been marked by two different teachers.
7 is being followed by a police car.

E 1 were built
2 be finished
3 been attacked
4 been taken
5 be posted
6 be made
7 were being loaded
8 are being typed

Unit 27

A 1 has her food delivered.
2 had the meat cut
3 has her hair cut
4 had his eyes checked.
5 will have her blood pressure checked.
6 had her car serviced.
7 are going to have the gutters replaced

B 1 They always have their carpets cleaned there.
2 I must have the tyres checked.
3 I ought to have a new key made for the front door.
4 I don't think I can afford to have our flat painted.
5 I had my watch mended there last week.
6 My husband had his eyes tested there last winter.
7 have that coffee stain removed.

C 1 Peter had his driving licence taken away by the police.
2 Paula had her bike stolen from the garage.
3 Fiona had her glasses broken.
4 John had his clothes torn in a fight.
5 Jane had her flat burgled at the weekend.
6 We had our electricity cut off because we had forgotten to pay the bill.

Unit 28

A
1. to go
2. playing
3. to buy
4. to take
5. repairing
6. to visit
7. talking
8. to help
9. to pay
10. to live
11. talking
12. to go

B
1. gave up studying
2. enjoy doing
3. deserve to pass
4. refuses to listen
5. keep studying
6. offered to help
7. promised to study
8. want to talk
9. stop asking
10. dislike listening
11. seem to think
12. need to study
13. have to find

C
1. to buy
2. to open
3. meeting
4. to phone
5. taking
6. washing
7. to finish
8. to feed
9. to invite

Unit 29

A
1. is an appliance for boiling water.
2. is an instrument for measuring temperature.
3. is an appliance for cleaning carpets.
4. is an appliance for keeping food cold.
5. is an instrument for seeing things in the distance.
6. is an instrument for measuring speed.
7. is an appliance for keeping food frozen.
8. is a tool for making holes.

B
1. A: What does Mary want the money for?
   B: She wants the money for a train ticket.
2. A: What does Philip want the flour for?
   B: He wants the flour for a cake.
3. A: What did Bill go to the butcher's for?
   B: He went to the butcher's for some sausages.
4. A: What does Helen want the polish for?
   B: She wants it for her shoes.
5. A: What did Alison go to the library for?
   B: She went to the library for a book on India.
6. A: What did Jane phone Ann for?
   B: She phoned Ann for some advice.

C
1. She wants the money to buy a train ticket.
2. He wants the flour to make a cake.
3. He went to the butcher's to buy some sausages.
4. She wants the polish to clean her shoes.
5. She went to the library to borrow a book.
6. She phoned Ann to get some advice.

Unit 30

A
1. Ann taught Mary to drive last year.
2. Don't worry! Tomorrow I will/I'll persuade my father to see a doctor.
3. The boss has forbidden his staff to wear jeans in the office.
4. Last Sunday, John invited Sheila to come for lunch.
5. Next year the teachers will allow/ are going to allow the students to use calculators in exams.

B
1. to come home early.
2. to work quicker.
3. to do our best in the game.
4. to come to her party next Saturday.

C
1. she would like him to stay.
2. she helped him to finish.
3. she/he advised him to stay in bed.
4. she allows them to go to late-night parties.
5. she reminded him to phone.

D
1. The driver let the old man travel on the bus without a ticket.
2. Jack made his younger brother wash the dishes.
3. I don't let people smoke in my house or in my car!

E
1. Diane watched Tom prepare the sandwiches.
2. We felt the ground shake.
3. Did you see Brian leave early?

Unit 31

A
1 What is Peter like?
2 What are Anna's parents like?
3 What does Tom look like?/What is Tom like?
4 What does Eva look like?/What is Eva like?
5 What are Bob and Tom like?
6 What does Susan look like?/What is Susan like?

B
1 What does a double bass sound like?
2 What do kiwis smell like?
3 What do kiwis taste like?
4 What does a double bass look like?
5 What do kiwis feel like?

C
1 Who does your sister like?
2 What are Paul's brothers like?
3 What does Jane like for breakfast?
4 Who are you like?
5 What is Mary's husband like?
6 What sports do you like?

D
1 What is John's flat like?
2 How was your boss yesterday?
3 What is a squash racquet like?
4 How is your sister?
5 What is Portugal like?

Unit 32

A
1 Are Tim and Jenny going to Oxford tomorrow?
2 Has Philip ever been on television?
3 How many photos did they take yesterday?
4 Where does your sister work?
5 Do you have a shower every morning?
6 What shall I bring when I come to see you tomorrow?
7 Who lives in that big house across the street?
8 What did Ted say to Bill?
9 Would you like to come on holiday with us?
10 Where is Ann living at the moment?

B
1 What does Jane have for breakfast?
2 Who did you see at the station?
3 Which does Mary prefer, tea or coffee?
4 What are you studying at university?
5 Which of these two books are you buying?
6 Who are they inviting to their party?

C
1 When is Lucy going to come?
2 Whose car did they borrow?
3 How long have they lived here (for)?
4 How many compact discs has Michael got?
5 How does Pam go to work?
6 Why did they stop working?
7 Whose is that bicycle?
8 How far is the coast (from here)?

D
1 a Who is Jack going to help?
   b Who is going to help Susan?
2 a How many prizes did John win?
   b Who won three prizes?
3 a Which machine makes the boxes?
   b What does the machine in the corner make?
4 a Whose sandwiches did Mary eat?
   b Who ate Tim's sandwiches?

Unit 33

A
1 Ruth says that she goes jogging every morning.
2 Anna says that Jenny isn't studying for her exams.
3 Andrew says that he used to be really fat.
4 Jim says that he can't swim.

B
1 Jim said (that) he was staying with some friends.
2 Mike said (that) he had never been to Russia.
3 Ella said (that) Tom couldn't use a computer.
4 Jill said (that) everybody had to try to do their best.
5 Rachel said (that) Jane might move to a new flat.
6 Bill said (that) he would stay at home on Sunday.

C
1 Anna said that I could rely on her.
2 Susan said that you had been very kind.
3 Mary said that you were staying with her.
4 I said to Angela that I would help her with her homework.
5 The teacher said that we were making too much noise.
6 Mark said that you might come to my party.

D
1 She told him (that) she liked his paintings.
2 You told me (that) you liked that film.

3 Tom told Ann (that) he felt ill.
4 She told Bill (that) she was leaving.
5 I told you (that) I couldn't find it.
6 Mary told him (that) she would send the letter.
7 We told them (that) we would arrive at six.

Unit 34

A 1 Jane to do the homework soon.
2 Ann to buy a map.
3 Mrs Clark to see a doctor.
4 Bill to keep all the windows closed.
5 Paul to go home.
6 Bob to stay for supper.

B 1 I reminded John to phone Sally.
2 The teacher told the children to wash their hands.
3 Jane tried to persuade Tom to play the guitar.
4 Paul asked Mary to lend him her bicycle pump.
5 She warned the children to stay away from the water.
6 The policeman advised Mark to see a lawyer.
7 She told Alan to have a shower immediately.
8 I reminded Sally to take an umbrella.

C 1 Yes, and I told him not to be late.
2 Yes, and she warned her not to go outside the house.
3 Yes, and I told him not to forget the stamps.
4 Yes, and he warned them not to eat late at night as well.
5 Yes, and he told them not to go near the windows.
6 Yes, and she particularly warned me not to eat nuts.

Unit 35

A 1 if/whether .... .
2 Why ... ?
3 how many .... .
4 if/whether .... .
5 if/whether .... .
6 What ... ?
7 when .... .
8 why .... .
9 where .... .
10 if/whether .... .
11 Where ... ?

B 1 Does Jim often play football?
I wondered if Jim often played football.
2 What have the children eaten?
She wanted to know what the children had eaten.
3 Where is Mark going?
I asked where Mark was going.
4 When is the next bus?
We wanted to know when the next bus was.
5 Has Ann seen this film?
Tom asked if/whether Ann had seen this film.
6 How many students will come on the trip?
Sara wondered how many students would come on the trip.

C 1 if/whether he had worked since then
2 if/whether his sister gave him money
3 who else gave him money
4 if/whether he knew Steven Ellis
5 how long he had known him
6 if/whether he had seen Steven recently

Unit 36

A
1. an ... a
2. an ... a
3. an ... a ... an

B
1. the ... a
2. the ... a
3. a ... The
4. a ... the
5. the ... a
6. The ... a

C
1. an ... the ... the
2. a ... a ... a ... the ... a
3. a ... the ... a
4. the ... the ... the ... the ... the

D
1. a
2. a
3. some
4. an
5. The
6. some
7. the
8. the
9. the
10. A
11. the
12. a
13. a

E
1. Turn to chapter four.
2. Who knows the answer to question two?
3. I have to do the second sentence.
4. Now look at test two.

Unit 37

A
1. There is ... it is
2. There are ... they are
3. There are ... they are
4. There is ... it is

B
1. there was
2. there will be
3. there used to be
4. there have been
5. There may be

C
1. There were five of us.
2. There were six of them.
3. There were twelve of us.

D
1. It rained a lot last night.
2. There was quite a lot of fog at the weekend.
3. It's very cloudy this morning.
4. There was quite a lot of rain last week.

E
1. It takes a few minutes to cook an omelette.
2. A: How long does it take to make tea?
   B: It takes about 5 minutes.
3. It takes about 3 hours to bake bread.
4. A: How long does it take to cook a stew?
   B: It takes about 2 hours.
5. It takes about an hour to make a cake.

Unit 38

A
1. such
2. so
3. such
4. so
5. such
6. such
7. so
8. so

B
1. such
2. such an
3. such a
4. such
5. such a
6. such an

C
1. He is such a wonderful cook!
2. Those people are making so much noise!
3. He was/is so lucky!
4. She wears such pretty clothes!
5. They were so delicious!
6. It is such an unhealthy habit!
7. It was so easy!

D
1. so slowly that she didn't finish the exam.
2. so expensive that we didn't buy it.
3. so tired that he didn't go out.
4. so small that Peter couldn't see them.
5. so much food that I couldn't finish it.

Unit 39

A
1. for
2. about
3. with
4. at
5. of
6. in
7. of
8. with
9. at
10. of
11. with
12. on
13. at
14. of

B
1. A: Is their daughter good at school work?
   B: Yes, in fact she is brilliant at everything.
2. A: Why is Mr Bell's dog afraid of him?
   B: Because he is often cruel to it.
3. A: Is Jenny fond of classical music?
   B: Yes, she is very keen on Bach, for example.
4. A: Are you pleased with Peter's exam results?
   B: Yes, we are very proud of him.

C
1. of listening to their problems
2. of old books
3. talking to him
4. to getting up early
5. for its watches

D
1. It is not worth staying until the end of the conference.
2. Mary is very good at making people happy.
3. I am very interested in Jill's new ideas.
4. Tom is busy talking to the guests.

Unit 40

A
1. on
2. on … in
3. at
4. in … on … in
5. in … on
6. in … in

B
1. on
2. behind
3. next to/beside
4. in front of
5. between

C
1. into … out of … into
2. onto … into … off … onto

D
1. from
2. across
3. along
4. past
5. up
6. in front of
7. down
8. through
9. under

E
1. in April.
2. on 20th April.
3. on Monday.
4. in the morning.
5. at 10 a.m.
6. in the spring.

Unit 41

A
1. ago
2. from
3. for
4. since
5. When
6. How long

B
1. has happened
2. lived
3. died
4. has been

C
1. How long … continued … from
2. When did … ended … ago
3. since … have changed since

D 1 We haven't spoken to Jane for two weeks.
We last spoke to Jane two weeks ago.

2 Helen hasn't visited Rome for twenty years.
Helen hasn't visited Rome since she was a student.

3 We last saw Mary two years ago.
We haven't seen Mary for two years.
We haven't seen her since she got married.

E 1 When did … first met
2 How long … took … from
3 did … last … met
4 How long … has been … since

Unit 42

A 1 which bit me
2 who wrote to me
3 which crashed
4 who had won a lot of money
5 who has a big house in Scotland
6 who designed the new city library

B 1 that I had seen on TV.
2 that Jane made.
3 that Mary sent me
4 that my sister wrote.
5 that I met
6 that my brother wants to buy.

C 1 who has visited so many different countries
2 who interviewed me
3 whose wives have just had babies
4 whose book won a prize last week
5 who complain all the time
6 whose car had broken down

D 1 -
2 -
3 who/that
4 that
5 that
6 who/that
7 -

Unit 43

A 1 The sun, which is really a star, is 93 million miles from the earth.
2 John F. Kennedy, who died in 1963, was a very famous American President.
3 Charlie Chaplin, who was from a poor family, became a very rich man.
4 The 1992 Olympics were held in Barcelona, which is in the north-east of Spain.
5 We went to see the Crown Jewels, which are kept in the Tower of London.

B 1 Football, which first started in Britain, is now popular in many countries.
2 Margaret Thatcher, who was the Prime Minister of Britain for 11 years, studied science at university.
3 Michelangelo, who lived until he was 90, is one of Italy's greatest artists.
4 The Nile, which runs through several countries, is the longest river in Africa.
5 Gandhi, who was born in 1869, became India's nationalist leader.
6 Elephants, which are found in Africa and India, live to a great age.

C 1 Madonna, whose parents were born in Italy, is a famous American singer.
2 Bill Clinton, whose wife is a brilliant lawyer, became President of the USA in 1993.
3 Sebastian Coe, who was a successful English runner, is now a politician.
4 Catherine of Russia, who ruled for over 30 years, made many important changes.

D 1 Maria sang and played the guitar
2 Sousse
3 The coach stopped at a petrol station
4 the news

Unit 44

A 1 Mary was tired so she went to bed.
2 I couldn't sleep because of the heat.
3 Jill doesn't eat apples because she doesn't like them.
4 The streets were crowded because there was a football match.
5 I'll give Jane a key in case she gets home before me.

B 1 in case she's at home.
2 because I want to lose weight.
3 because his passport was out of date.
4 so I'll take a book to read.
5 in case there is a power cut this weekend.
6 because his wife was ill.

C 1 so that everybody would know our new address.
2 so that they can keep their clothes clean.
3 so that they can keep in contact with each other.
4 so that she can be nearer her work.

D 1 Last week, my brother lent me £20 so that I could buy some new shoes.
2 Last month, the Government passed new traffic laws so that fewer people will have accidents.
3 Our school has opened a new library so that we can have more books.
4 Ann always writes everything in her diary so that she doesn't forget her appointments.
5 Last Friday, we left home early so that we could avoid the morning traffic.

Answer key to exit test 1

1	b	12	c	23	b	34	b
2	b	13	b	24	c	35	b
3	c	14	b	25	b	36	c
4	c	15	c	26	c	37	a
5	a	16	a	27	c	38	a
6	c	17	c	28	c	39	a
7	c	18	c	29	b	40	c
8	c	19	b	30	b	41	c
9	b	20	c	31	b	42	a
10	b	21	b	32	c	43	a
11	a	22	a	33	a	44	a

Answer key to exit test 2

1	b	12	c	23	b	34	b
2	c	13	a	24	c	35	b
3	c	14	b	25	c	36	c
4	c	15	c	26	a	37	a
5	a	16	c	27	b	38	a
6	a	17	b	28	b	39	a
7	c	18	c	29	a	40	a
8	c	19	c	30	a	41	a
9	c	20	a	31	b	42	a
10	b	21	a	32	a	43	c
11	c	22	b	33	c	44	b

Index

The numbers in the index are unit numbers. They are not page numbers.